Transcending Ego:
Distinguishing Consciousness from Wisdom

Bibliotheca Indo-Buddhica Series No. 214

Transcending Ego: Distinguishing Consciousness from Wisdom

(Tib. *namshe yeshe gepa*)

of

Rangjung Dorje, *The Third Karmapa*

With a Commentary by

The Venerable Khenchen
Thrangu Rinpoche
Geshe Lharampa

Translated by Peter Roberts

Sri Satguru Publications
A Division of
Indian Books Centre
Delhi, India

Sri Satguru Publications
A Division of
Indian Books Centre
24/4, Shakti Nagar, Near Dena Bank,
Delhi-110007

Email: ibcindia@vsnl.com
Website: http://www.indianbookscentre.com

First Indian Edition; Delhi, 2001

ISBN 81-7030-704-X

We would like to thank Peter Roberts for translating the root text and Thrangu Rinpoche's commentary. We would also like to thank Gaby Hollmann for transcribing and editing the teachings, and Sarah Harding for painstakingly checking the manuscript. We would also like to thank Pönlop Rinpoche for his advice on the manuscript.

Note

Technical words are italicized the first time that they are used to alert the reader that their definitions may be found in the Glossary.

We have not used Sanskrit diacritics. Instead we have spelled words as they appear in the *Handbook of Tibetan Culture*.

Similarly, to help the Buddhist practitioner, the Tibetan words are given as they are pronounced, not spelled in Tibetan. With every section of Tibet pronouncing words differently, the pronunciations are rough approximations. The actual spelling of Tibetan words are, however, given in the Glossary of Tibetan Terms.

We also use the convention of using B.C.E. (Before Current Era) for "B. C." and C.E. (Current Era) for "A. D."

Published by sunil Gupta for Sri Satguru Publications, a division of Indian Books Centre, 24/4, Shakti Nagar, Delhi-110007, India and printed at D.K Fine Art Press Pvt. Ltd., New Delhi-110 052.

The Table of Contents

Rangjung Dorje, the Third Karmapa (1284-1339 C.E.)

Editor's Foreword

Two and a half millennia ago the Buddha proposed that all our happiness and all of our suffering are due to one thing: our mind. After his own realization he spent the rest of this life giving teachings on how we ourselves can work with our mind to achieve complete peace, nirvana, or enlightenment.

The basic way of working with mind is through meditation. The Buddha began by teaching tranquillity (Skt. *shamatha*) and insight (Skt. *vipashyana*) meditation which are practiced by Buddhists all over the world. This path, called the sutra path, is a very steady and gradual path. Except in the case of a few exceptional individuals, it takes many lifetimes of meditation to achieve enlightenment using the practices of the sutra path. To practice the Buddhist teachings, regardless of sect or style, one should begin by practicing the accumulation of great merit, the development of a pure conduct, and engaging in shamatha and vipashyana meditation. There are many excellent books on the sutra path by great Theravadin teachers, Zen masters, and Tibetan lamas including Thrangu Rinpoche's *The Practice of Tranquillity and Insight*.

Another path leading to enlightenment is the Vajrayana path. If one applies oneself with great effort to the practice of the Vajrayana, it is possible to achieve enlightenment rapidly. As pointed out many times by Thrangu Rinpoche, the goal of enlightenment, is exactly the same for all paths. The choice is in the method one wants to pursue. Both the sutra and Vajrayana methods have been extensively practiced in Tibet. One of the most important Vajrayana meditations is the meditation of the mahamudra or "great seal." Looking directly at the mind and seeing what is or is not there is the method. To understand mahamudra meditation, it is important to identify the mental process. The examination of the nature of mind, how thoughts arise, where they dwell, and disappear show how the mind works.

This text on consciousness and wisdom is a detailed map of what is perceived when one engages in this process of looking into the mind. Rangjung Dorje begins with a description of the eight mental consciousnesses and describes each in terms of what it does and how it leads us to perceive our world incorrectly. Because these eight consciousnesses cause us to see the world in a deluded way, we continue to live in samsara and this causes us to continue to experience unhappiness, frustration, dissatisfaction, and emotional upheavals. Rangjung Dorje, being one of the great Buddhist thinkers of his time, in this text brings together the Abhidharma literature of the Theravadins, the Mahayana doctrines on emptiness, the Mind-only writings of the Cittamatrins, and the practice of examining mind directly of the mahamudra. After this description of the eight consciousnesses he describes how these are transformed into the five wisdoms that are present in the mind at the time of the attainment of enlightenment.

Central to all discussion to the nature of reality in the Mahayana and Vajrayana levels of Buddhism is the concept of emptiness. Emptiness (Skt. *shunyata*) is the fundamental characteristic of matter and this is treated slightly differently in two traditions in Tibet. One tradition, the Shentong tradition, to greatly simply holds that there is Buddha-nature which pervades all sentient beings and it is this *tathagatagarbha* which is the potential for all sentient beings to reach Buddhahood. The other Rangtong tradition holds that everything is empty of inherent existence and so Buddha-nature cannot exist in everyone as a permanent quality. The latter Rangtong position is mainly supported by the Gelug school of Tibetan Buddhism (who take a very academic stand based on the works of Nagarjuna), while the Shentong school is mainly supported by the Kagyu and Nyingma schools who emphasize meditative practice. The delineation of the Shentong and Rangtong view is given in more detail in Hookam's *The Buddha Within*. This treatise by Rangjung Dorje is an important text of the Shentong view, which differs slightly from the Rangtong presentation of consciousness and wisdom. In addition Rangjung Dorje held a few views which were different from the traditional Cittamatra view, so the presentation, particularly of the actual consciousness into wisdoms may appear to contradict the teachings of some other teachers. Thrangu Rinpoche reviewed the section of the transformation of consciousnesses into wisdoms to make sure the text conformed exactly to what Rangjung Dorje had proposed.

The Treatise Distinguishing Consciousness from Wisdom was written by the eminent scholar, the Third Karmapa, Rangjung Dorje. Like most other texts on mahamudra practice, this treatise is not in the form of a scholarly thesis, but in the form of a spiritual song, or *doha*. A spiritual song distills the realization of the Vajrayana practitioner in verse, each line usually having nine syllables. This particular text is very compact and comprises only thirty-six verses. In the nineteenth century the great scholar, Jamgon Kongtrul, wrote a longer commentary on this treatise to help clarify its meaning. Thrangu Rinpoche consulted this commentary of Jamgon Kongtrul as he taught on this spiritual song.

In the Tibetan tradition a student first memorizes these root verses as a part of his or her religious studies. The student then requests a lama, known not only for his or her scholarly accomplishment and understanding of the text, but also for the lama's realizations, to give a lengthy line-by-line commentary on the root text. We are pleased to offer here both a translation of this great vajra song and a commentary by Thrangu Rinpoche, an eminent scholar of Buddhism who possesses the above qualities. With this text the Western student of Buddhism can have the experience of being able to study a profound text with a commentary by an excellent scholar of Buddhism in the same way that Tibetan students in the Buddhist monasteries of Tibet have studied this text for the past millennium.

Distinguishing Consciousness from Wisdom is an important text on psychology, as well as Buddhist philosophy. Rangjung Dorje arrives at conclusions about how the mind works which are far different from what modern Western psychology would suggest. To illustrate this, I will briefly summarize the arguments of the text, not in the order presented in the text, but in a Western framework.

First, Buddhist meditators have reported since the first century of our era that everything is "empty." Physicists in the twentieth century has come put with a similar conclusion. We are told in modern physics that the solid matter is no longer little hard balls of protons, neutrons, and electrons, but are actually made up of energy patterns. The physicist Bohm has said so poetically, "matter is crystallized light." It is well known that solid objects are actually 99.99% "empty" space and that the atoms that make up solid objects are actually moving at incredible speeds. In a recent book Michael Talbot presents information from experiments in modern physics that suggest this vast universe we live in is a giant hologram. This may be far fetched, but it explains in physical terms why everything is connected and how some clairvoyant individuals, including many realized lamas, can know what is happening thousands of miles away or even years into the past or future. So Rangjung Dorje in this text begins his exposition by refuting the view that a god or gods created the solid universe and that the universe is actually empty.

Second in the argument is that Buddhist meditators have known from at least the fourth century of our era that it is the human mind, or more specifically, human awareness that has made the material of this universe seem to be solid to us. They point out that individuals have reincarnated for thousands of lifetimes and in each of these lives they have had extensive experience with material objects and that this experience has been stored in their mind (in what is called the eighth consciousness). In Western science the scientific proof in reincarnation lies in the methodology of past life regression and it is too bad that hard scientific investigation has yet to be made to demonstrate whether individuals in this lifetime can recall events and facts about their previous lives that was not gained by any source in this lifetime. Who better to make the argument for reincarnation than the author of this spiritual song, the Karmapa? The Karmapa for the past sixteen lifetimes has written a letter a few years before he has died and in this letter which is not opened until several years after his death it gives his name as a child, the name of his parents, and where they can find him. So far the letter has always been accurate demonstrating that he understands reincarnation at a level far beyond any of us ordinary beings.

Since human beings have had similar experiences, they therefore "see" and experience the world in a similar fashion. To use Michael Talbot's analogy, our mind has created the solidity of the hologram so that when we run into a brick wall, which is really an energy projection like a hologram, we bounce off it and are hurt. While we may argue with the holographic theory, Amit Gaswani, an author of a widely used textbook in quantum mechanics has take data from physics and summarized this in his *The Self-Aware Universe: How Consciousness Creates the Material Universe*. So we see that when

Rangjung Dorje describes how mind creates the universe based on his study of the Cittamatra school, he is not far from what modern physics is exploring some 700 years later.

Third, the alaya consciousness, first described in the fourth century by the Cittamatra school of Buddhism, stores all our impressions and karmic latencies and this makes it possible for us to function. If we look at a piece of metal that is of gold and shows a man seated cross-legged touching the ground, we immediately think, "a statue of the Buddha." But how did we know it was the Buddha or even who the Buddha was? We must have stored somewhere in our mind some previous experience where someone had told us who the Buddha was. This then is one function of the alaya consciousness. Penfield, a Canadian neurologist working with epileptics has presented evidence that we store every sensory impression we experience in the brain. Rangjung Dorje citing the Cittamatrins goes much further than this and says that the alaya consciousness stores impression over many lifetimes which obviously places the alaya consciousness outside of the brain.

Fourth, the alaya consciousness has been treated by all meditators as being empty of nature and when we feel that we possess a mind, this mind is merely a continuity of an every changing stream. This means the mind for Buddhists is not a permanent self in the Hindu sense or a soul in the Christian sense. This consciousness does not only store these impression from many lifetimes, but it also stores the karmic latencies of these experiences. This fact is very important for the meditator because if the eighth consciousness didn't store these latencies, there would be no cause and effect for our actions, and essentially we could do anything we wanted to do with no fear of consequences (except for what the authorities found out). However, there is karma so we as Buddhist on the path must engage with great diligence to have only positive impressions and latencies enter our alaya consciousness. When we meet the Dalai Lama or some other realized person, we can almost feel the goodness and compassion radiating from them. This is not because they have been doing some special practice, but rather that they have been diligently working with their mind to produce positive karma.

Sixth, these latencies or impression leave the alaya consciousness in two ways: first, when we dream these karmic latencies appear to the mental consciousness and the mental consciousness takes them to be real phenomena; second, when sense impressions from our sense faculties reach the mental consciousness, the mental consciousness combines these with the latencies from the alaya consciousness and these appear real and solid to us, although outer phenomena is actually not solid and real.

Seventh, with great diligence of having only positive impressions and latencies enter the alaya consciousness and with strong meditation, we can actually purify this alaya consciousness to the point that our ordinary consciousnesses transform into the five wisdoms of enlightenment. Then we are no longer bound by our material circumstance and have actually transcended this samsara that we have bound as in for countless lifetimes. At this point a great master such as Milarepa can put his hand through solid objects because he has completely realized that they are in fact empty. It is only our latent impressions over hundreds of lifetimes that have made external phenomena solid and "real" for us.

Clearly, this summary is a very cursory account of Buddhist psychology. What this text does point out is why Eastern and Western psychology is so difficult to reconcile because these two psychologies rely on such different assumptions. It also shows how modern and relevant Rangjung Dorje's text is even though it was written seven hundred years ago.

Thrangu Rinpoche's commentary on this text was given at two different occasions: at the Namo Buddha Summer Seminar in Oxford, England in September, 1989, and at the Namo Buddha Winter Seminar in January of 1990 in Nepal. Rinpoche gave a different presentation at each which emphasized some points in one teaching and other in the other one. We have combined the most detailed explanations from each of these teachings to give the most thorough commentary of this very important work.

Clark Johnson, Ph. D.

Translator's Preface

Prior to the time of the Buddha (c. 490-410 B.C.E.) the *Brahmanas* and the earliest *Upanishads* of the Vedic tradition in India presented enumerations of the constituents that comprised an individual's mind and faculties, such as the eight pranas described in the *Brdharanyaka Upanishad*: the prana of breath, eye, speech, tongue, ear, body, mind (*manas*), all of which arose from and were reabsorbed into an underlying *atman* (soul or self).

The Buddha, who referred to and refuted the *Brdharanyaka Upanishad*, denied the existence of the underlying atman, but enumerated the constituents of the empirical individual in his doctrine of five aggregates (*skandhas*), or the six conscious-nesses.

All the early Buddhist traditions that developed from the third century B.C.E. onwards, preserved the teaching of six consciousnesses. In particular, a systematizing doctrine based on the Buddha's sutras attempted to present a numeric delineation of the constituents of existence. This was known as the Abhidharma traditions such as the Vaibhashika considered certain Abhidharma texts to be the words of the Buddha. The Tripitaka or "Three Baskets" were formed through conjoining the Abhidharma to the collection of the sutras together with the Buddha's teachings on monastic rules, the Vinaya. Other philosophical schools, such as the Sautrantika, however, refused to recognize the canonical authenticity of the Abhidharma, which was given commentarial status only.

All Tibetan Buddhist traditions recognize the supremacy of the Sautrantika amongst the early schools of Buddhism; therefore, there is no Abhidharma section in the Kangyur, the Tibetan canon of the Buddha's words. All Abhidharma texts are found only in the Tengyur, the Tibetan translations of Indian Buddhist treatises and commentaries. The principal treatise in this canon is the *Treasury of the Abhidharma* (*Abhidharmakosha*) by Vasubandhu (fourth to fifth centuries C.E.).

The Madhyamaka (Middle Way) tradition, which was promulgated especially by Nagarjuna (second century C.E.) also taught the six consciousnesses. Later Madhyamaka masters such as Candrakirti (seventh century) and Shantideva (675-715 C.E.), who are referred to by Thrangu Rinpoche in this book, maintained this view, denying the validity of the two additional consciousnesses introduced by the Cittamatra (Mind-only) school promulgated especially by Asanga (fourth century) and by his younger brother Vasubandhu in his later Mahayana works, such as *The Thirty Verses,* a key source for Rangjung Dorje's *The Treatise Distinguishing Consciousness and Wisdom.*

The eighth century witnessed the rise of a syncretism of Madhyamaka and Cittamatra, such as that taught by Shantarakshita. Shantarakshita came to Tibet 762 C.E. and was instrumental in establishing Buddhism there. As a result of this unification of differing views, scholars began to divide the Buddha's teachings into those in which the meaning is explicit, and those in which the meaning is implicit. In the latter category, the apparent meaning was, therefore considered to be expedient. This new method of classification allowed scholars to consider the body of the Buddha's teachings as a unified hierarchy of what were otherwise regarded as contradictory views.

In addition, by the mid-eighth century, the tantra was well established. This introduced a system of the five dhyana buddhas, with corresponding sets of elements, afflictions, and wisdoms. The numerical equivalence with the five aggregates facilitated a teaching of the transmutation of specific skandhas to corresponding wisdoms. This teaching is found, for example, in the eleventh century terma, the *Bardo Todrol*, better known as *The Tibetan Book of the Dead.* In this system all eight consciousnesses are included within the aggregate of consciousness, and so all eight transform into dharmadhatu wisdom. In turn each of the other aggregates transforms as follows: form transforms into mirror-wisdom, the aggregate of sensation into equality wisdom, the aggregate of identification into discriminating wisdom, and the aggregate of mental activity into accomplishment wisdom. Rangjung Dorje's text, however, presents a less-well known alternative. According to this text, the aggregate of consciousness alone transforms into all five wisdoms.

Rangjung Dorje (1284-1339) was the third in the lineage of Karmapa reincarnations, the supreme hierarchs of the Karma Kagyu school, that commenced with Dusum Khyenpa (1110-1193). He composed *The Treatise Distinguishing Consciousness and Wisdom* in 1323 C.E. based particularly on the writings of the founders of the Cittamatra school, Asanga and Vasubandhu.

The commentator to this text, Jamgon Kongtrul (1813-1899), was a prolific commentator, compiler, and editor of Buddhist teachings, especially of the Karma Kagyu tradition. He wrote commentaries for all three of Rangjung Dorje's texts: *The Profound Inner Meaning, The Treatise Elucidating Buddha-Nature* and this work *The Treatise Distinguishing Consciousness and Wisdom* Jamgon Kongtrul's commentary on the latter text is entitled *An Adornment for Rangjung Dorje's Thoughts.* It is this commentary which served as the basis for Thrangu Rinpoche's teaching on the Third Karmapa's text.

In 1959, in order to escape from the holocaust of Chinese Communist oppression unleashed at that time, the eighth Thrangu Rinpoche (born in 1933) had to leave Thrangu Monastery in east Tibet. He fled to Sikkim and later became abbot and principal scholar at Rumtek monastery in Sikkim, where Rangjung Dorje, the Sixteenth Karmapa (1924-1981), had established his seat in exile. Subsequently, Thrangu Rinpoche founded Thrangu monastery and also the Namo Buddha retreat center in Nepal. Since 1979 he has toured the world extensively, establishing Buddhist centers, and is most recently consecrated Vajra Vidya Institute which will become a center for teaching Buddhism at the place where the Shakyamuni Buddha give his first teaching.

Peter A. Roberts

Table 1

The Five Aggregates of Consciousness (Skt. skandha, Tib. pung po)

The Aggregate	The Sanskrit	The Tibetan*
1. form	rupa	gzugs
2. feeling	vadana	tshor ba
3. identification	samjna	'du shes
4. mental formation	samskara	'du byed
5. consciousness	vijnana	rnam shes

**The Tibetan words are given as they are spelled, not pronounced.*

Chapter 1

An Introduction to the Text

There are four major traditions of Tibetan Buddhism: the Kagyu, Sakya, Nyingma, and Gelugpa. Each school has its own particular approach. The Gelug school, for example, emphasizes learning and scholarship producing great scholars, whereas the Kagyu school emphasizes meditation and is known, therefore, as the *Drubgyu* or "practice lineage" school. The principle meditation of the Kagyu lineage is the *mahamudra*[1] or 'great seal'. The mahamudra instructions came from Saraha (ninth to tenth century C.E.), Tilopa (928-1009 C.E.), and Naropa (956-1040 C.E.). They taught through the method of brief *spiritual songs* or *dohas*. These spiritual songs do not give detailed information on Buddhism but use poetical imagery to introduce the listener to the nature of the mind. Spiritual songs express these practice instructions in the form of poetry. They are very brief and direct and are very beneficial to the mind. Although they do not provide thorough background information on the teaching; they do give direct instructions on recognizing the nature of the mind.

Gampopa (1079-1153 C.E.), the Tibetan master who founded the monastic order of the Kagyu school, unified the teachings of the mahamudra tradition with the scholastic and monastic *Kadam* tradition of Atisha (982-1055 C. E.). Gampopa taught that the study of Maitreya's *Uttaratantra* would be a great help for comprehending the mahamudra instructions on experiencing the nature of one's mind.

Gampopa's principal pupil, Dusum Khyenpa (1110-1193 C. E.), was the First Karmapa and founded the Karma Kagyu school, which has since been governed by successive Karmapa rebirths. The Third Karmapa, Rangjung Dorje (1284-1339), composed a text entitled *The Profound Inner Meaning.* In it he described the *subtle channels* and *subtle winds* that exist within the body and how these winds and channels are the basis for the practice of meditation.[2] He also composed two other very short texts: *The Treatise Distinguishing Consciousness and Wisdom*, which is the text we are concerned with here and a summary of the *Uttaratantra* entitled *A Treatise Elucidating Buddha-Nature*. Rangjung Dorje said that if we can understand the *Uttaratantra* with these two short texts, then we will be able to understand mahamudra meditation.

THE EIGHT CONSCIOUSNESSES: AN OVERVIEW

A Treatise Distinguishing Consciousness and Wisdom assumes that we have a certain familiarity with the doctrine of the eight consciousnesses. Therefore, before explaining the treatise itself, I shall give a brief description of the eight consciousnesses.

The first teachings given by the Buddha were those now practiced primarily by Theravadin Buddhists and the path is called the *Hinayana* path.[3] These teachings enumerated six different kinds of consciousness. First, there are five consciousnesses associated with the five physical sensory organs: the visual consciousness of the eye, the aural consciousness of the ear, the olfactory consciousness of the nose, the gustatory consciousness of the tongue, and the tactile consciousness of the body. These *five sensory consciousnesses* directly perceive the external objects of visual forms, sounds, smells, tastes, and body sensations without any conceptual differentiation of these phenomena into good and bad, pleasant and unpleasant, and so on. They are the nonconceptual consciousnesses of direct perception.

The sixth consciousness is the *mental consciousness*, which engages with the perceptions of the other five consciousnesses. In the Buddhist science of epistemology and logic, called the *pramana*, the mental consciousness is defined as a conceptual consciousness. It is the mental consciousness that defines a visual perception, for example, as being good or bad, large or small, and so forth. So first, an object is perceived by the eye and this perception is first apprehended by the visual consciousness. This then passes on to the mental consciousness, which then thinks, "This is good," or "This is big." This categorization goes on, of course, for the perceptions from the other four sensory consciousnesses.

The mental consciousness does not have the ability for direct perception. So, for example, if we see a bell, the visual consciousness produces a visual image of the bell, but doesn't apprehend the name "bell" or its characteristics. The mental consciousness, however, apprehends a mental image of the bell, not as a visual image, but is aware of the name "bell" and its specific characteristics. For example, the visual consciousness can see only one side of a door. The mental consciousness, however, can join many instances of perceiving the door and conceive a mental image of the front, back, inside, and outside of the door.

The five external sensory consciousnesses are like a mute who can see. Although a mute person can see everything, he cannot describe what he has seen. The mental consciousness, on the other hand, is said to be like a blind person who can speak: he is able to describe things, but he cannot directly perceive them.

The Buddhist teaching of the six consciousnesses refuted the pre-Buddhist doctrines that asserted the existence of a single consciousness, or self. These nonBuddhist theories held that there is only one consciousness, although it may seem as if there are many. They gave the example of a monkey inside a house with six windows. Sometimes, the monkey looks out the east window, sometimes out the north window, then out of the west window, and so on. An observer on the outside might think that there are six monkeys in that house, even though in fact there is only one. This was to explain how one consciousness could process information from the five sensory and the mental consciousness.

The Buddha and his followers did not accept this view. They countered that there were six distinct consciousnesses, each with its own particular characteristics. The Buddha taught that if there were only one monkey inside a house, when it looked out of an eastern window, for example, then all the other windows would be empty. But when we see something with our eyes, our ears do not become deaf. When we listen with our ears, our eyes do not become blind. We can see, hear, and smell simultaneously, within the same instant, so there must be six separate consciousnesses.

The six consciousnesses were described by the Buddha to be *aggregates* (Skt. *skandhas*), not single units. For example, when we perceive different colors, such as yellow, red, and white one consciousness does not perceive all these colors; instead a different visual consciousness perceives each color. Similarly, there are also different visual consciousnesses for perceiving triangles, squares, and circles. In the same way, an aggregation of auditory consciousnesses is itself an aggregation of a multitude of momentary consciousness perceiving different sounds. Similarly, a collection of tactile consciousnesses experience the sensations of hands, feet, and other body parts simultaneously.[4] The sixth mental consciousness is also made of many consciousnesses, because the mind can conceive of many different things such as past, present, and future.

The six consciousnesses are impermanent. A visual consciousness does not last from morning to evening. The visual consciousness of an image arises for only an instant; it then ceases and is immediately followed by another visual consciousness that lasts for only an instant. Therefore these six consciousnesses are aggregates of successive momentary consciousnesses.

As well as being impermanent, the five sensory and the mental consciousness are classed as temporary because they are not always present. For example, when one closes one's eyes, there is no longer a visual consciousness perceiving visual images. The mental consciousness is also characterized by the quality of *luminosity* (Tib. *salwa*),[5] and clearly perceives the object, while the seventh and eighth consciousnesses are not as vivid and apparent. The seventh and eighth consciousnesses are classed as being 'ever-present but unclear' while the first six consciousness are classed as 'temporary, but very vivid'.

In the *Mahayana* teachings the Buddha described two additional consciousnesses. The seventh consciousness is called the afflicted consciousness and it functions basically as clinging to a self. This consciousness is very subtle in that it does not need to specifically think, "Is this me?" Instead, it is continuously and latently present, clinging to a self whether a visual, auditory, gustatory, olfactory, or kinesthetic perception is taking place. This contrasts with the mental consciousness where the feeling of self is very conscious and discernible. The afflicted consciousness is a neutral obscuration and in itself is neither positive nor negative. It does not create good or bad karma. However, the belief in a self directly opposes the wisdom of realizing *egolessness*.[6] This affliction is the principle obstacle that must be removed to attain liberation.

The eighth consciousness is called the ground consciousness; it too is an aspect of luminosity and understanding that is ever present. No matter what kind of sensory perception occurs, this underlying continuity of consciousness is there. The eighth ground consciousness is the basis, the ground, for all the other consciousnesses. It can be analyzed in terms of mind and mental events. Five mental events arise from the ground consciousness: form, feeling, identification, formation, and consciousness.[7] In the case of the seventh consciousness there are nine mental events: the above five as well as clinging to self, attachment to self, pride in self, and ignorance in relation to self. These mental events are like the transformations or the movements of the consciousnesses. When we look thoroughly and directly at the mind, we can identify each of these consciousnesses.

Among the eight consciousnesses, the mental consciousness is the most important. The visual consciousness may see a image which may or may not be beautiful; the ear consciousness may hear a pleasant or unpleasant sound and so on, but the mental consciousness decides if the sensory perception is beautiful or ugly. The liking of a perception brings about joy, attachment, and gives rise to the *afflictions* or disturbing emotions (Skt. *kleshas*).[8] Experiencing an unpleasant sensory perception brings suffering and a disturbance of mental clarity. When meditating, we use our mental consciousness to calm and pacify the mind. Meditation pacifies all sensations and experiences of happiness and suffering, of attachment and aversion. When all sensations have been pacified, the mind is clear and peaceful. We then rest in this clear and peaceful state. This completely natural and true state of the mind is ultimate wisdom. When this state of wisdom is attained, all the eight consciousnesses are transformed into the five wisdoms.

This text describes the consciousness, explains how they function, and defines the nature of the five wisdoms in detail; therefore, it is called *The Treatise Distinguishing Consciousness from Wisdom*.

THE TITLE

The Treatise

The body of Buddhist literature can be divided into two categories: the discourses given by the Buddha himself, which are called the "Buddha's words," or *ka* in Tibetan, and the subsequent commentaries written by the Buddhist masters, or *shastra* in Sanskrit. The word *shastra* was translated into Tibetan as *tenchö*. The Tibetan word *chö* means "to correct;" a shastra corrects ignorance, error, and delusion in the mind and changes them into wisdom. The shastra accomplishes this by teaching (Tib. *ten*) the true nature clearly. When the truth is understood, the mind is automatically corrected. Thus, a treatise is called *tenchö* in Tibetan, meaning "correction through teaching." This text is, therefore a treatise, a *tenchö*, that clearly teaches the nature of consciousness and wisdom in order to dispel our ignorance and delusion.

Distinguishing

Rangjung Dorje differentiates consciousness from wisdom in this treatise by classifying them according to their respective natures. He does this in order to provide us with the knowledge necessary for successful meditation.

Consciousness

It is due to consciousness that we do not have ultimate knowledge. The Tibetan word for consciousness is *namshay*. This term was derived from the Sanskrit *vijnana*. The Sanskrit word *vijnana* means "complete knowing" with the first syllable *vi*, meaning "total," and the second syllable *jnana* meaning "knowledge."

Consciousness does not creat ignorance. It is a state of luminosity or intelligence of mind. However, what should be seen (i.e. the true nature of phenomena) is not perceived by consciousness, and what is should not be seen (i. e. false appearances) are seen by consciousness vividly. This results in a state of delusion that prevents the realization of ultimate wisdom.

from Wisdom

The Tibetan word for wisdom is *yeshe*, which is a translation of the Sanskrit word *jnana*. The Sanskrit term, however, can also mean ordinary knowledge, the equivalent to the Tibetan word *shepa*. Therefore, the Tibetans translated *jnana* as 'ultimate wisdom' and added *ye* which means "primordial," to *she* thus forming *yeshe* which means "primordial wisdom."

The reason that we meditate is to transform our mind: to change our ignorance into wisdom, our erroneous beliefs into true knowledge, from being under the influence of the negative emotions to being free from these negativities. So we are trying to change our impure state into a pure state. The impure state is the mind; the pure state is also mind. They are both mind, but there is a great difference between these two. The impure states are termed consciousnesses (*namshay*), and the pure states are termed wisdoms (*yeshe*). If we can clearly understand the difference between consciousness and wisdom, then our subsequent meditation practice will be free from error and delusion. This treatise on *Distinguishing Consciousness from Wisdom* is, therefore, very important for the practice of meditation.

THE HOMAGE

1. I pay homage to all the buddhas and bodhisattvas![9]

The treatise commences with the homage and the commitment to compose the text. Traditionally, from the time that early Buddhist masters composed shastras in India until the present time, Buddhist treatises have begun this way. Rangjung Dorje therefore begins his treatise with a homage to worthy recipients who are the buddhas and the *bodhisattvas*.

The Buddha's teachings are divided into three sections: the Vinaya (the instructions on correct conduct), the Sutras (the words of the Buddha), and the Abhidharma (a systematic classification of the teachings). A specific homage is associated with each of these three different types of teachings. This treatise belongs to the category of *sutra teachings*, which is principally concerned with meditation, and the traditional homage for a sutra text is "I pay homage to all the buddhas and bodhisattvas." Thus this homage is paid to the Buddha, who taught the perfect dharma, and also to the bodhisattvas who are the practitioners of those teachings. This homage is made to ensure that there will be no impediments to the completion of the text and to ensure that it will benefit many people.

Rangjung Dorje pays homage to the Buddha, who taught how to pacify all mental afflictions and sensations. Rangjung Dorje also pays homage to the bodhisattvas, those beings who practice the Buddha's teachings. So by showing respect and devotion in the buddhas and bodhisaṭtvas one's confidence in the teachings grows. By having a firm confidence in the teachings, one will practice them, and by practicing the teachings, one will achieve the goal of Buddhahood.

THE COMMITMENT TO COMPOSE THE TEXT

2. I gained a thorough understanding through hearing the teachings
And contemplating them.
I then resided in solitude, in order to engage
In the process of meditation. I shall describe here,
The kind of realization that arose at that time.

This verse expresses Rangjung Dorje's commitment to compose the text. On an explicit level, Rangjung Dorje describes the process that resulted in his writing this text. Implicitly, these lines instruct us to do as he has done. It is as if he is saying, "This is what my followers should do in the future." Rangjung Dorje was an emanation of *Avalokiteshvara*, yet he humbly describes himself as an ordinary being. He says that he did not know how to practice properly, so it was first necessary to gain an understanding of words of the Buddha and the commentaries. Unable to do this by himself, he studied with a master in order to gain the understanding that arises from listening to the teachings.

We shouldn't believe in something just because the Buddha, or some great scholar or *lama* says so. We need a very clear and profound conviction that the Buddha's teachings are correct and this is gained by using analysis and our own intelligence. Therefore, after our teacher has taught us the path, we should analyze and think about the teachings, and so gain the second type of understanding, which arises from contemplation.

The understanding based on listening and contemplation is not enough—this alone cannot transform our mind. This final transformation is accomplished by meditation. How do we meditate properly? This is described with the words "I then resided in solitude." Having developed complete certainty in the teachings, Rangjung Dorje then meditated on the teachings in order to change his mind. He meditated in a solitary place so all the movements of his mind and the unstable thoughts would disappear and transform into wisdom. Through his meditation he was able to completely understand these questions and realized how important it would be for others to understand the nature of consciousness and the five wisdoms. So he composed this text. Rangjung Dorje teaches us by example that we too should learn to see the nature of consciousness and wisdom, through hearing and contemplating the teachings. Then we should follow this meditation in solitude.

We can't achieve realization on our own. If we meditate with our inadequate capabilities, we won't be able to develop genuine meditation. Instead we need the help of someone who has had the experience of meditation: that someone is the Buddha. He has taught about the nature of meditation, given the methods of meditation, and taught the purpose of meditation. We must first listen[10] to the teachings of the Buddha, then we must understand the teachings by contemplating them. After developing a definite understanding, we then have to meditate on the teachings. So we must do all three together—listen, contemplate, meditate in order to progress.

The Buddha taught that we must meditate to achieve realization. For example, we cannot convince someone that molasses is sweet by repeatedly telling them that it is sweet. Even though the person may understand our words, until that person personally tastes it, he or she will not have the experience of the sweet taste. It is the same for *Dharma*; we can listen to the teachings for a long time and contemplate them, but without meditation we cannot actually experience them. If, however, we taste the molasses, we will have the actual experience of its sweetness. Similarly, if we practice meditation properly by following the correct path and receiving the proper instructions, we will experience the Dharma. In the *King of Samadhi* sutra it says that to meditate properly, one has to first receive instruction on meditation, and one must understand these instructions. There is a story of a *rishi,* a sage, who meditated for twelve years without achieving any real results. He died and was reborn a cat. The reason he was reborn a cat, not a human, was that he had not received the proper meditation instructions.

Consequently, the Buddha said we must listen to the teachings and contemplate them before we meditate on them. He said that he himself had also listened to the teachings, contemplated them, and then meditated on them. As his followers, we should do the same.

PART I:

The Eight Consciousnesses

Table 2 (Part I)
The Fifty-One Mental Factors
(Skt. chaitta, Tib. sems byung)

Five Omnipesent mental factors (sarvatraga, kun 'gro)

1. feeling	vadana	tshor ba*
2. discerment	samjna,	'du shes
3. intention	chetana	sems pa
4. contact	sparsha	reg pa
5. mental engagements	manaskara	yid la byed pa

Five determining mental factors (viniyata, yul la byed pa)

6. aspiration	chhanda	'dun pa
7. belief	adhimokshha	mos pa
8. recollection	smriti	dran pa
9. stabilization	samadhi	ting nge 'dzin
10. superior knowledge	prajna	shes rab

Eleven Virtuous Mental Factors (kushula, dge ba)

11. faith	shraddha	dad pa
12. shame	hri	ngo tsha shes pa
13. embarassment	apatrapya	khrel yod pa
14. detachment	alobha	ma chags pa
15. non-hatred	adveshha	zhe sdang med pa
16. non-bewilderment	amoha	gti mug med pa
17. jours effort	virya	brtson 'grus
18. suppleness	prasrabdhi	shin tu sbyangs pa
19. conscientiousness	apramada	bag yod pa
20. equanimity	upekshha	btang snyoms
21. non-harmfulness	avihimsa	rnam par mi 'tshe ba

Chapter 2

The Mind as the Source of Delusion and Nondelusion

THE ERRONEOUS VIEWS OF OTHERS

3. There are those, who believe that the three realms and all beings,
Are a creation arising from themselves, or from another,
From both, or from no cause.
There are those who state that there is a creator:
Gampo-Cha, Shiva, Brahma, or Vishnu,
Or that there are external atoms,
Or truly existing imperceptible matter,
That has created the self and the world.

In the past there have been many different teachers from many different traditions who have presented views on how to understand the nature of phenomena. They have taken views much different from Rangjung Dorje's view that external phenomena are created by the mind. We need to understand why these teachings are incorrect to have a clear understanding of how phenomena arises. Therefore Rangjung Dorje begins with a refutation of inaccurate theories of how phenomena arises.

There are external appearances in the world and the beings within it. The Buddhist tradition describes the world in terms of *three realms*: the desire realm, the form realm, and the formless realm.[11] Where did these realms come from? Some philosophical schools state that things or phenomena originate from the self, some state that things originate from other, and some state things originate from self and other, and some schools state that things originated without any cause.

The latter view was held by the Carvakas, a tradition that stated that the world had no cause whatsoever. They illustrated their view with the example that peas are round, but no one has rolled them into that shape; thorns are sharp, but no one has sharpened them. Similarly, they contend that the entire world occurs naturally, without any cause. Some other traditions believed that there was a creator who made this world. This is the view of the *Bon* religion, the religion that was already present in Tibet before the introduction of Buddhism in the seventh century. These Bonpos stated that "Fortune" or *Cha* in Tibetan is the cause for the eventual attainment of prosperity, and is also the creator of everything in the world.

In India there were three pre-Buddhist religions that believed in a creator: Shaivism, Brahmanism, and Vaishnavism. The followers of Shiva believed that Shiva had thought or dreamed, "this world is necessary," and this thought created the world. The followers of Brahma believed that he gazed with his four faces into the four directions, and from this he had created the entire world. The Vaishnavites believed that Vishnu, being very skillful and intelligent, created this world out of his own skill.

It should be clear that nothing arises without a cause as claimed by the Carvakas. If this were the case, then there would be no point in planting seeds since there is no cause or reason for them to spout. If plants were created by Shiva or a god then there would be no point in planting seeds because the god would decide what to let grow. It is reasonable therefore to say that things are not created by gods because all things need a cause.

Among the Buddhist schools there were different views on how outer phenomena was created. When the Buddha first began teaching, he gave teachings that were compatible to the understanding of his students. These became the Hinayana teachings and were intended for *shravaka* practitioners. In these teachings, the Buddha said that there was no creator, instead everything was made up of minute particles like atoms. This was the view of the Vaibhashika school. Another Hinayana teaching of the Buddha was that there were small invisible particles which were "hidden" from mind and from these the self and the external world were created. This was the view of the Sautrantika school. Although these two schools taught there was no creator, their views were still not completely correct.

WHAT THE BUDDHA TAUGHT

4. The unique, Omniscient One taught that
Those three realms are purely mind.
They are not derived from themselves, nor from that which is other,
Not from both, nor from the absence of a cause.
All phenomena arise through interdependence.
They are, by their own nature, empty,
Utterly free of being single or multiple,
Utterly free of being falsehood or truth,
Like the moon's reflection upon water and so on.
Knowing this, the Buddha taught it to beings.

The Omniscient One (the Buddha) would teach according to the level of his students. He would often teach two different meanings: the *definitive meaning* and the *provisional meaning*. When the Buddha taught the definitive meaning, which describes the true nature of phenomena, he explicitly stated that all appearances in the three (the desire, the form, and the formless) realms were mind. He said there was no external creator and that everything is created by, arises in, and is perceived by mind alone.

There were four major schools of Indian Buddhism: the Vaibhashika, the Sautrantika, the Cittamatra (Mind-only) and the Madhyamaka (Middle-way) schools. There are actually two different Cittamatra schools: one which says that appearances are mind and nothing else, and the second that says that appearances were created by mind in the first place. This second school then taught that the three realms of existence, that is, all phenomena did not arise due to a self, or through others, or through no cause at all; rather it asserts that phenomena arises through interdependence or *dependent origination*,[12] with one phenomenon dependent upon another, without a creator being involved.

A simple example of this is given in Kamalashila's *The Stages of Meditation* which says that if one has a two-inch incense stick and a four-inch incense stick, the four-inch stick is clearly the longest and this is agreed upon by everyone. But if one then adds a six-inch stick and takes away the two-inch stick, then suddenly the four-inch stick is the shorter stick. So being long or short, big or little, right or left, etc. always depends on the interdependence with other objects rather than on its nature[13] or the inherent quality of the object itself. The incense stick is not short or long in itself, that quality occurs only through dependence upon other phenomena and through the analysis by the mind. Therefore the Cittamatra or Mind-only tradition taught that because of this, the mind alone is the basis for all appearances.

The mind is the source for everything, without a creator deity being necessary, because it is the mind that creates all actions, and therefore all karma. All happiness and unhappiness, anger, attachment, love, and compassion arise from the mind and nowhere else. So the mind is the source of all *samsara* and *nirvana.*

In a sutra the Buddha said, "Oh bodhisattvas, the three realms are only mind." That may make us think, "What about these houses, mountains, and fields that I see? They are all external to my mind!" However, when we see houses and fields in dreams, we think of them as being external objects that are not created by the mind, even though they are nothing other than projections of our mind. All that we see when we are awake too, is nothing other than a creation of the mind.

We see objects such as houses, trees, and mountains on a gross level. In fact, when we look carefully, we realize that nothing exists as a single entity. Everything is actually made up of many components. For example, when we look at our hand, our mind conceives of it as a "hand." Actually, it is made up of skin, flesh, bones, and different fingers. When we examine the thumb more closely, we see it is composed of a nail, skin, and different joints, etc. There is really nothing to look at that can be considered even the thumb, yet our mind says "thumb." It is the same way for everything else: nothing exists as a single entity because it can always be broken down to smaller particles. Even if it can be broken down to the smallest particle, we can analyze that particle and discover that this smallest particle has four sides—a north, south, west, and east. Therefore even the smallest particle cannot be defined as a singularity. Yet all these things appear as single conceptual formations in the mind. They arise in the mind and therefore their source is the mind.

HOW RANGJUNG DORJE GAINED REALIZATION

5. From what source does this
Delusion and non-delusion arise?
I have understood the nature of dependent origination,
In the same way that one sees one's own reflection in a mirror,
And knows that there is fire because there is smoke,
And I shall clearly describe it here.

Buddhists believe everything appears in the mind, just like an image appears in a mirror. Everything arises through dependent origination similar to a reflection in a mirror. For a reflection to occur one needs a visual image and then also a mirror that reflects this image. It is the interdependence between the image and the mirror that allows us to see the image in the mirror. This example illustrates interdependence on the *ultimate level.*[14] Similarly, when we see smoke, we know that this is dependent upon fire so that when we see smoke, we know there is a fire. This illustrates interdependence on the *conventional* or relative level.

Rangjung Dorje gained knowledge and wisdom from listening to the teachings and the understanding that comes from contemplating them. Rangjung Dorje also received the actual practice instructions and teachings on the sutras and *tantras* from a guru in order to develop the understanding that comes from receiving the teachings. The sutras are the Buddha's Mahayana teachings and the tantras are the Buddha's *Vajrayana* teachings. He also received the teachings of the shastras, which are the commentaries on the Buddha's teachings. Rangjung Dorje received all these teachings and contemplated them. Having realized the essence through study and contemplation, he experienced the source of samsara and nirvana. Therefore, he was able to see this clearly, just like one sees one's reflection in a mirror.

Rangjung Dorje describes his realization in terms of the two truths. On the ultimate level he realized the source of delusion and non-delusion, that is, the nature of phenomena. On the conventional level, he realized how phenomena arise through interdependence. Having attained these realizations, he described the consciousnesses and wisdoms.

Table 2 (Part II)
The Fifty-One Mental Factors

Six Root Afflictions (mulaklesha, rtsa nyon)

22. desire	raga	'dod chags
23. anger	pratigha,	khong khro
24. pride	mana	nga rgyal
25. ignorance	avidya	ma rig pa
26. doubt	vichikitsa	the tshom
27. afflicted view	drishti	lta ba nyon mongs can

Twenty Secondary Afflictions (upaklesha, nye nyon)

28. wrath	krodha	khro ba
29. resentment	upanaha	'khon 'dzin
30. concealment	mrakshha	'chab pa
31. spite	pradasha	'tshig pa
32. jealousy	irshhya	phrag dog
33. avarice	matsarya	ser sna
34. deceit	maya	sgyu
35. dishonesty	shathya	g yo
36. self-importance	mada	rgyags pa
37. harmfulness	vihimsa	rnam par 'tshe ba
38. non-shame	ahrikya	ngo tsha med pa
39. non-embarassment	anapatrapya	khrel med pa
40. lethargy	styana	rmugs pa
41. agitation	auddhatya	rgod pa
42. non-faith	astraddhya	ma dad pa
43. laziness	kausidya	le lo
44. non-consciousniousness		pramada bag med pa
45. forgetfulness	mushhitasmritita	brjed nges pa
46. distraction	vikshhepa	rnam par g. yeng ba
47. non-introspection	asamprajanya	shes bzhin ma yin pa

Four Changeable Mental Factors (aniyata, gzhan 'gyur)

48. contrition	kaukritya	'gyod pa
49. sleep	middha	gnyid
50. examination	vitarka	rtog pa
51. analysis	vichara	dpyod pa

Chapter 3

All Appearances Are the Mind

THE FIVE SENSORY CONSCIOUSNESSES

6. The five sensory consciousnesses create afflictions
Because of holding and rejecting
Forms, sounds, smells, tastes, and tactility.
What are these sensory objects?
If the wise examine well, they will know that
Nothing, such as atoms and so on, exist externally,
As anything other than cognition.

The five sensory consciousnesses of the eye, ear, nose, tongue, and body perceive the five sense objects of visual forms, sounds, tastes, smells, and body sensations. Basically, all sights, sounds, and smells are neither good nor bad, but some are perceived as being good and are accepted and some are perceived as bad and are rejected. These perceptions of pleasure and displeasure give rise to the afflictions or disturbing emotions (Skt. *kleshas*) which then cause all the suffering and illusory appearances of samsara.

If those who are endowed with wisdom properly examine the cause of all this suffering and illusion by wondering, "What are these sensory objects?" They will discover that although thoughts of beauty and ugliness, good and bad, and so on, are associated with the sensory objects, these qualities are not actually inherent in the objects sensed. Instead these qualities are in the mind because there is no sensory object that exists outside that mind.

There are four conditions that are necessary for a perception of an external object to occur which results in a disturbing emotion. The first condition, called the 'causal condition,' is the condition that the ground (eighth) consciousness and the afflicted (seventh) consciousness have to be present.[15] The second condition, called the 'primary condition,' is the condition that the actual sensory faculty and its consciousness of the eye, the ear, the nose, the tongue, or the body must be present. The third condition, called the 'objective condition,' is the condition that the external sensory object such as a sight or sound or smell must be present. Without this sensory object the sensory consciousness cannot arise. For example, the ear consciousness will arise because of a sound and a nose consciousness will arise because of a smell, and so on. So for these five sensory consciousnesses to arise there has to be an object that can be perceived by the sensory faculty. The fourth condition, called the 'immediate condition,' is the condition of the continuum of the mind. Since the mind is a succession of individual instants, there's a thought for one instant, then there's another thought the next instant, this continuum must also be present.

The result of these four conditions coming together is that we have a sensory experience that results in the perception of something which is either pleasant or unpleasant or neutral. If we perceive something as pleasant or beautiful, we think that it is good, and we are pleased, and we then develop the disturbing emotion of desire or attachment. If we perceive something as unpleasant or ugly, we will dislike it, which will gradually develop into the disturbing emotion of aversion or anger. If we see something that we think of as neutral, one will not see the true nature of the object, and we will respond to it with the disturbing emotion of stupidity or ignorance. We can see from this that all the negative emotions come about as a result of perceiving an object that is automatically identified as good, bad, or unimportant.

We experience happiness or unhappiness based on our perception. But even when we experience something as pleasant and enjoys it, we will later experience suffering from this object; happiness is impermanent and will eventually become a source of suffering because we will lose this desired event or object. This suffering then comes from the four conditions: the eight consciousnesses, the continuum of mind, the five senses, and their objects.

REFUTING THE ERRONEOUS VIEW THAT THE SENSORY OBJECTS ARE NOT THE MIND

7. *If the substance of those sensory objects were other than consciousness,*
They could not both be a single entity.
A non-manifesting, immaterial awareness
Does not create material substance.
Therefore, a relationship where the latter arises from the former, could not exist.
With this view that sensory objects are other than consciousness,
It will become illogical for sensory objects to appear from consciousness,
Because they would have no connection.

Before explaining how all external phenomena are mind, Rangjung Dorje refutes the view held by many that external reality is not the mind. He uses the argument that if external phenomena were other than the mind, then external phenomena would have a different nature[16] than the mind. The view he is refuting is the view held that external phenomena are matter, and that the nature of consciousness is awareness.

If mind and external phenomena had completely different natures or essences, then there could be no connection or relationship between them: objects wouldn't be able to arise out of the consciousness that perceived them. The only way there could be a relationship between objects and their perceiver would be if they were to have the same nature: objects would be able to arise out of the consciousness that is perceiving them. The relationship between matter and consciousness must be one of two kinds: they must be between things of the same essence or between things of a different essence. An example of having two same natures is like seeing an elephant in a dream: we see a dream elephant, and both the nature of the elephant and the nature of the perception are our mind. An example of two things having different natures is like seeing an elephant while waking. In this case, there must be an instant between the elephant and the consciousness perceiving it, because they cannot arise at exactly the same time; therefore, it is impossible for them to have a relationship other than cause and effect.

WHY EXTERNAL PHENOMENA ARE MIND[17]

8. Therefore, all these various appearances,
Do not exist as sensory objects which are other than consciousness.
Their arising is like the experience of self-knowledge.
All appearances, from indivisible particles to vast forms, are mind.
This means, that if nothing exists externally and separately,
Brahma and the rest, could not be creators.

When we learn that external objects are only mind, and are not separately existing things, we might answer, "Well, I can see them. They are made out of matter; therefore, they are different from mind, which is not made up of matter but has the quality of clarity or awareness. So, mind and external objects are completely different things. One is solid matter and the other is clarity." To refute this argument we can use the previous example of a hand. We say, "Oh, I see a hand." But if we investigate more closely, we see a thumb, an index finger, a middle finger, ring finger, and a little finger, skin, flesh, and bones. We then ask, "Where is this hand that I see?" In fact, the hand is just a mental fabrication. We then look at the thumb and say, "I see a thumb." But the thumb consists of the first, second, and third joints, and so on, and therefore, also is made up of many different parts. We know that none of these parts are the thumb, and ask, "Well, where is the thumb?" There is only one answer: there is no actual thumb. We see something and think we see a hand, but in fact there is no real hand there. It is only a mental fabrication. The same analysis applies to the fingers, a mountain, a house, or to any other external object.

An explanation of the line in the verse which says "Their arising is like the experience of self-knowledge" will be given with the next verse.

We may hold the position that all external phenomena are composed of collections of real, minute particles and these indivisible particles are gathered together to make external phenomena that we perceive. When we, however, examine these small particles more closely, we find that we cannot divide them into the smallest particle because each particle can be divided into still smaller particles. So there is no such thing as a particle that everything is made up of, and there is no reality in this external phenomena. So we must conclude that all external appearances arise from mind.[18]

We will never find an external object separate from our mind. We see things as being separate, because, since the beginning of time, which we have spent in samsara, we have been habituated to the idea that phenomena exist externally. All external phenomena, from the smallest, indivisible particle to the largest mountain, appear from the mind alone. Many traditions say that the world and all beings inhabiting it were created by Brahma, Shiva, and Vishnu; they mistakenly assert that gods created the smallest particles which we might call atoms. However, everything we experience, whether pleasant or unpleasant arise from our mind through the power of karma, and is not created by gods.

EXPLANATION OF THE MENTAL CONSCIOUSNESS

9. The relationship between the mental consciousness and mental phenomena,
Is like the experience of a dream.
The mind focuses on phenomena
And becomes attached to them.
But they are devoid of any true reality.

Although we may intellectually agree with the statement that all objects are only experienced by mind and don't exist due to external causes, we do not actually believe this. We believe that there are two separate things: external objects and an inner consciousness perceiving them. Although we believe them to be separate, the Buddha taught that these events are not external, but are only mind. Ordinary logic doesn't agree with this. For example, if we were to say that this book that we are reading is our mind, we would think, "No, that is not true. The book was made by a printer, and did not come from our mind; it is an external object." But when we dream, we also see external objects; yet none of them have an independent external existence; they are all just mental creations. In the same way, all external appearances that we perceive are created by our mind, and do not have any independent existence.

The five sensory consciousnesses perceive sensory objects or events directly as mental images of visual forms, sounds, smells, tastes, and bodily feelings. These are then perceived by the sixth consciousness, which is the mental consciousness. But the mental consciousness does not perceive the sensory objects directly, but as mental events. These mental images are sometimes termed *dharmas*, which is translated as "phenomena," meaning the purely mental phenomena that appear to the mind. The relationship between the mental consciousness and these mental phenomena is not direct, but rather like that experience in a dream. In a dream the mental phenomena appears to the sixth consciousness which takes it as being real. A similar process occurs in a dream in which all the appearances in a dream arise internally to the mind and are conceived of as being external phenomena. There is a strong attachment to these images being external phenomena both is the dream and in waking.

The subject of *Pramana* describes mental consciousness as having two aspects—an external orientation and internal orientation. The external orientation is when the mental consciousness becomes attached to the sensory form that is perceived by a sensory consciousness. For example, when there is a sound, a mental consciousness engages that sound. This is the external orientation of the mental consciousness.

The mental consciousness with an internal orientation is called 'self-knowledge', which is the mind being aware of itself. The pramana tradition states that "One's own mind is not concealed from oneself." We have to ask someone else what they are thinking about, but we know exactly what we ourselves are thinking. This isn't because our mind is looking at itself as if it were something else. There is no dualism of something that is seen and something that is doing the seeing. We don't have to wonder, "What am I thinking?" because we can clearly perceive it. This internal orientation of mental consciousness which looks[19] at the mind itself is called *rang rig*[20] in Tibetan, and means "self-knowing." Externally oriented mental consciousness is conceptual and inferential. When we look at something, for example, we can compare it with previous sights, we can analyze it to determine its qualities, and we can name it. In contrast, internally oriented mental consciousness of looking at mind's own nature is nonconceptual and must be perceived directly. As ordinary (unenlightened) persons we can by inference understand that the mind is capable of seeing its own nature, but we do not have the direct experience or recognition of this self-knowledge. To recognize this self-knowledge directly, we have to engage in meditation to directly see the essence of mental consciousness. After we have done that, we should abide in this non-conceptual state.

If we do not recognize self-knowledge, but indulge in the externally oriented aspect of mental consciousness, then we will become involved in the usual flow of thoughts and remain in a state of delusion. But if we can reject the externally oriented consciousness and rest in self-knowledge, we will have effective meditation. Therefore, it is taught, "Rest like an infant seeing a temple." When we bring a baby into a temple, the baby directly sees all the objects and images, but it doesn't think, "Oh, that is a throne, that is the Buddha," instead, it has a direct experience of the temple. During meditation, we should have this direct experience without thoughts and concepts, and experience self-knowledge.

In terms of meditation, the important consciousness is the sixth mental consciousness. When we are doing a meditation involving visualization, some of us believe that we should see the visualization as clearly as we see a regular object; however, we are using the mental consciousness, while in normal vision we use a visual consciousness. Since a mental consciousness perceives the meaning of an object, it cannot perceive a clear picture in the way that the visual consciousness can, so we cannot expect a visualization to be as clear as seeing an ordinary object. Also in tranquillity (*shamatha*) and insight (*vipashyana*) meditation we use the sixth consciousness; we observes all the movements of thoughts in our mind. It is the sixth consciousness we are training in this meditation.

THE MIND IS EMPTY[21]

10. These six consciousnesses,
The appearances of sensory objects and of beings,
The attachment to a self, cognition
Whatever appearances are manifested
Are not created by anything which is other than themselves.
They are not created by themselves,
Nor created by both self and other,
Nor by the absence of both.

In the graduated path of meditation it is first taught that all external phenomena are mind. This has been covered in the previous chapter and now we come to the discussion of how the mind itself, the six consciousnesses, have no inherent reality and are empty in nature. The verse begins by stating that there are no external appearances, only the internal six consciousnesses to which there appear the external sensory objects, the belief in self, and the internal thoughts and feelings. These events or appearances are analyzed in the classic four-fold logic of Nagarjuna used in the *Perfection of Wisdom* (Skt. *Prajnaparamita*) teachings. These internal and external appearances to mind are: (1) not created from themselves, (2) nor are they created from something outside themselves, (3) nor are they created from both themselves and other, (4) nor are they created from neither themselves nor other. In other words, they are empty by nature.

Rangjung Dorje now describes how all external things are mental manifestations. We may wonder if this is the same viewpoint as the Cittamatra (Mind-only) school who assert that all external phenomena are mental manifestations and that phenomena have no true existence; only the mind truly exists, which is why they are called the Mind-only school. Rangjung Dorje, however, goes further, and teaches that the mind is birthless, has the quality of being empty, and possesses luminosity. The text shows that external things have no true existence, and when we investigate our mind, we discover that it also has no true existence. An example is given by our usually saying that there is a mountain over here and a different mountain over there. But there is no definite mountain "here" and a mountain "there" because the mountain over "there" becomes the mountain "here" when one goes over to the other mountain. Therefore mountains don't have an intrinsic nature of being here or there; everything is instead interdependent with "here" depending on "there" and vice versa.

Similarly, the known and the knower also depend upon each other. When something is known, there is a knower; where there is a knower, something is known. If nothing were known, there would be no knower, because the knower depends on what is known for its existence. If external objects have no true existence, then the mind will have no true existence either. If visual forms have no true reality, then visual consciousness has no reality; if sounds have no reality, then auditory consciousness has no reality and so on. If external phenomena have no true reality, then the six consciousnesses have no reality; if sense objects have no reality, then the actual senses themselves, and the sense organs have no reality; if the sense organs have no reality, then the consciousnesses that arise from them have no reality. Therefore, if both external phenomena and internal consciousnesses have no true reality, then neither a self nor clinging to a self has a true reality.

Even though nothing has a real nature, things do obviously appear. We see a car and we open the door and climb in and drive along the highway. A vast variety of appearances do appear and do have an effect on us so we wouldn't, for example, deliberately drive our car into a wall. These appearances are part of relative or conventional reality and they appear to mind because mind has luminosity. When this luminous aspect of mind which is awareness or knowingness is impure, we have consciousnesses. When this luminosity is pure, we have wisdom. However, neither this luminosity nor this wisdom has any true reality on the ultimate level. Thus, all appearances have a clarity of manifestation and a nature which is devoid of reality.

To summarize it is said that external phenomena and inner consciousnesses are not created by (1) the self, (2) something other than the self, (3) both self and other, nor (4) neither self or other. Thus all external phenomena and the consciousnesses have no true inherent nature.

THE SCRIPTURES ON THE EMPTINESS OF MIND

11. Therefore, as the Victorious One has taught,
All samsara and nirvana are just mind.

That all external phenomena are mind and that mind is empty can be developed through logic as this treatise has done, or it can be established by reading the scriptures of the Buddha. The Buddha taught that the mind is responsible for us attaining Buddhahood and mind is also responsible for us wandering in samsara. The Buddha has said that the mind is like an artist who paints whatever he wants. The mind uses the *five mental aggregates* of form, feeling, identification, activity, and consciousness to create whatever is perceived in the world.

Saraha (9th century C.E.) in India who was one of the eighty-four *mahasiddhas* practicing the mahamudra said that mind is like the seed of everything.[22] While we reside in our confused state in samsara, everything that we want can be obtained from the mind and when we achieve Buddhahood, all the enlightened qualities and wisdoms are also obtained by mind. Therefore when we use our mind properly, we can obtain both the happiness of samsara and the happiness of nirvana. In this way the mind is like a *wish-fulfilling jewel.*[23]

Why is it that we are not always happy? It is that through countless lifetimes we have become thoroughly habituated to the false belief or delusion that external appearances are inherently existent or "real" and are distinctly separate from our mind.[24]

This process of how mind creates phenomena is elaborated in a sutra in which the bodhisattva Manjushri is asked by a deva,[25] "Has the external world not been created by someone?" and Manjushri replied, "Son of deva, the external world was not created by anyone. It was not created by Bhrama, Shiva and so on. The entire world was created only through latent karmic imprints.[26] When these imprints developed and increased, they formed the earth, the stones, the mountains, and the seas. Everything was created through the development or propagation of these latent karmic potentials." Then the deva asked, "How can all external forms arise out of latent karmic imprints? All these mountains, oceans, the sun and moon are so solid and so vivid. How can they arise out of latent karmic imprints in the mind?" Manjushri replied, "These things arise through the power of development and the propagation of thought."

We have many examples of this in the East. For example, there was an old lady meditating on the visualization of herself being a tigress and she concentrated and focused so clearly that others actually saw her as an actual tigress. Also there is a well-known practice of monks to reduce their sexual desire by visualizing human bodies as containing all kinds of impure substances such as pus and urine. Sometimes other individuals can see these monks as having rotten and putrid bodies. While these two examples are very small ones occurring over brief periods of time, we can imagine how large objects such as mountains can be produced by the minds of millions and millions of sentient beings since beginningless time.

Table 3

The Eighteen Elements or Constituents of Mind
(Skt. dhatu, Tib. khams)

The six objects:

1. visual forms	rupa	gzugs*
2. sounds	shabda	sgra
3. smells	gandha	dri
4. tastes	rasa	ro
5. objects of touch	sparsha	reg bya
6. mental phenomena	dharma	chos

The six sense organs:

1. eye sense organ	chakshur-indrya	mig gi dbang po
2. ear sense organ	shrotrendriya	rna ba'i dbang po
3. nose sense organ	ghranendriya	sna'i dbang po
4. tongue sense organ	jihvendriya	lce'i dbang po
5. body sense organ	kayendriya	lus kyi dbang po
6. mind sense organ	mano-indriya	yid kyi dbang po

The eight consciousnesses

1. eye conscious.	chakurvijnana	mig gi rnam par shes pa
2. ear conscious.	shrotravijnana	rna ba'i rnam par shes pa
3. nose conscious.	ghranenvijnana	sna'i rnam par shes pa
4. tongue conscious.	jihvavijnana	lce'i rnam par shes pa
5. body conscious.	kayenvijnana	lus kyi rnam par shes pa
6. mental conscious.	manovijnana	yid kyi rnam par shes pa
7. afflicted conscious.	kleshavijnana	nyon mongs rnam par shes pa
8. ground conscious.	alayavijnana	kun gzhi rnam par shes pa

* *Tibetan given as spelled, not pronounced.*

Chapter 4

How the Eight Consciousnesses Cause Delusion

The *Treatise that Distinguishes Consciousness from Wisdom* presents an outline of the whole treatise in a brief form in the first eleven verses. We have reached the point in the treatise where each of these points is covered in more detail.

THE SUMMARY OF THE EIGHT CONSCIOUSNESSES

12. The causes, conditions, and interdependence,
Have been taught by the Buddha to be the six consciousnesses,
The afflicted mental consciousness, and the ground consciousness.

Causes, conditions, and interdependence is necessary for things to arise in the mind; they don't appear without reason. For example, growing a flower requires a seed, the conditions of water, sunlight, soil, and the like. Finally, interdependence is necessary; cause and conditions must be in the right amount, and occur at the right time. If a flower has too much water or not enough sunlight, it will not grow. Likewise, birth in samsara doesn't just happen; its causes and conditions and their interdependence must be present for all the illusionary appearances of samsara to arise.

The six consciousnesses are literally called the six accumulations, and resemble the teaching of the five skandhas. The six consciousnesses are not a single entity, are impermanent, and do not possess an inherent reality; they are instead an accumulation of many moments of consciousness.

As an example of their impermanence, we assume that we have a single visual consciousness from morning to evening. Upon close examination, however, we discover that a visual consciousness only arises when a sensory object contacts the sensory organ. When this circumstance doesn't occur, the visual consciousness ceases. When we see a red color, a visual consciousness perceiving red arises and ceases. A visual consciousness arises for an instant and then ceases, allowing the next visual consciousness to arise and cease in the next instant. This process also applies to the other consciousnesses—an auditory consciousness perceives a loud sound and then a quiet sound, and so on, with consciousnesses continually arising and ceasing in a succession of instants.

The samsaric appearances that arise from these causes and conditions are of two kinds: common and individual. Some appearances are the result of identical causes created by many beings, so that something will be seen by everyone in common, such as everyone in a particular room seeing that it has two pillars. However, there are certain individual causes and conditions which result in beings having their own individual experiences of happiness and discomfort. For example, some people taste chili and think it's delicious, while others taste it and experience discomfort. Even though the flavor and the sensory organs of their tongues is the same, differing individual experiences occur. These different perceptions are due to different latencies that have been laid down in the ground consciousness. The latencies of different individuals are different making for different causes for the six sensory consciousnesses.

THE OBJECTIVE CONDITIONS OF THE CONSCIOUSNESSES

13. The six consciousnesses are dependent on objective conditions,
Which are the six sensory objects of form and so forth.

As previously mentioned, the arising of consciousness depends on four conditions: the objective condition, which is the sense-objects; the primary condition, which is the sense organs; the immediate condition, which is the immediate mentality that will be explained in conjunction with the seventh consciousness; and finally the causal condition, which is the eighth ground consciousness. In more detail, the first condition is called the object condition; images, sounds, smells, tastes, and tactile sensations are perceived. These make the five sensory objects and the sixth object is the phenomena arising in the mental consciousness. The sixth sensory objects are called "phenomena" because the image appearing to the mind is not the actual direct perception of, for example, a visual form. A visual form is not directly perceived by the mind, rather an image of the visual form appears. Similarly, when the mind conceives of a taste; there is no perception of the actual taste, instead an image of taste appears in the mind. None of the five objects are directly perceived by the mind. When an appearance of any one of the five objects arises in the mind, it becomes the sixth object. The six objects are the object conditions for the arising of the six consciousnesses.

These images alone would not be able to give rise to the six consciousnesses without a second condition, the primary condition, which are the actual senses themselves—the sense of the eye, the sense of the nose, the sense of the ear, and so on.

THE PRIMARY CONDITIONS OF THE CONSCIOUSNESSES

14. Their primary conditions are the six sensory objects,
Which are clarity endowed with form.

The primary condition or the main cause for perception are the sensory organs. These are often taken to be the eyes, the ears, the nose, the tongue, and the body. But these sensory faculties are not the actual physical sense organs themselves. Rather the *Abhidharma*, which describes the elements of mind in great detail, says that the senses are actually "the basis of the organs." As Rangjung Dorje says, "Which are clarity endowed with form." Clarity or luminosity is the faculty of knowing and shows the sense faculties have the power to perceive.[27] Jamgon Kongtrul gives the actual physical form of these faculties according to Tibetan medicine. The sensory faculty in the eye is said to be like a flax flower, which is blue in appearance. The sensory faculty of the nose is like a knot in white birch, like a hole, shaped similar to an ear. The sensory faculty of the ear is like a row of very fine copper needles. The sensory faculty of the tongue is like a moon split in half and laid on the tongue. The sensory faculty of the body is said to be smooth and permeates the entire body, except for the hair and nails.[28]

Thus the six consciousnesses arise as a result of the six sensory objects and six sense faculties;. together they add up to the *eighteen constituents of perception* (Skt. *ayatanas*) which are responsible for appearances arising in the three realms.

THE SOURCE OF THE SIX CONSCIOUSNESSES

15. Both faculties and objects arise from the mind.
This manifestation of sensory objects and faculties
Is dependent upon an element that has been present
Throughout beginningless time.

The five sensory consciousnesses being noncognitive perceive objects vividly because they do not discriminate between beautiful and ugly, desirable and undesirable, and so on. Nagarjuna compared these senses to an idiot who can see everything clearly, but cannot think, "this is good and that is bad." In contrast the sixth mental consciousness cannot directly perceive objects; it rather follows what is perceived by the sensory consciousnesses, and has a rough or vague idea of those perceptions of external forms. It is conceptual and conceives of phenomena as being, good or bad, similar or different, and so on.

Having established that there are sensory objects and sensory faculties, we may now ask, "Where did these external phenomena come from?" The answer is that all of external phenomena—houses, mountains, roads, and their perceptions—originated from the mind. They all arose out of the ground consciousness.

How is this possible? The answer lies in the fact that since beginningless time we have been perceiving sights, sounds, smells, tastes, and bodily sensations and these perceptions have been creating imprints or latencies in the ground consciousness. Habituation of having experienced a certain visual form will create a latency for that very form. Eventually, that latency will manifest from the ground consciousness as a visual form again, but it will be perceived as external to ourselves.

Everything the mind thinks occurs within the mind itself. As mentioned before, the closest analogy of this process is a dream. Although dream phenomena have no connection to external objects, we become attached to their mental images which are, in fact these imprints of latencies coming from the eighth consciousness. Because we think that dream phenomena and external objects are the same, we grasp at that thought. Apart from the grasping, there is no connection between phenomena experienced in mental consciousness and external objects. This is why it is said everything appearing to the five senses arises, in fact, only from mind.[29]

A BRIEF INTRODUCTION TO THE SIXTH AND SEVENTH CONSCIOUSNESSES

16. Though a sensory consciousness perceives an object
Its particular characteristics are known by the mental event of identification,
Which is dependent upon the mental consciousness:
The immediate mentality and the afflicted-mentality.

Briefly, there are the Cittamatrin or Mind-only school associated with Asanga and the Madhyamaka or Middle-way school associated with Nagarjuna. The Cittamatrins state that all phenomena are mind; the Madhyamakas state that all phenomena are empty. This text presents the information in terms of successive mahamudra meditation (in contrast to the methods of analytical meditation)[30] by first teaching that all phenomena are the mind, and then describing the empty nature of the mind.

It is easier to first recognize that the nature of all phenomena is the mind; having gained that direct recognition, we realize that mind itself is empty. Presenting the subject in this order facilitates direct recognition, whereas simply learning the Madhyamaka view that phenomena are empty logically makes it difficult to gain understanding. Thus Rangjung Dorje first teaches that all phenomena are the mind, and then teaches how the mind itself is birthless.

The sixth mental consciousness has no form and is called 'the intermediate consciousness' or the consciousness following immediately upon arising or immediately upon cessation. As soon as a sensory perception of form occurs, the mental conception of that form immediately arises. The other senses also have a mental conception immediately following perception. The sixth mental consciousness like the sensory consciousnesses, also exists in one instant and ceases in the next; mental consciousness that has ceased becomes the condition for the mental consciousness following in the next instant.

This verse introduces how the other consciousnesses fit in with the sensory consciousness in the process of perception. Even though the sensory consciousnesses perceive external sense objects, they are not recognized or perceived as a solid external object until this perceptual process reaches the mental consciousness and the object is identified. The mental consciousness, however, does not store a memory of all the objects—this comes from the seventh and eighth consciousness. The seventh consciousness is particularly mentioned and it has two aspects or functions: it serves as the immediate mentality which ensures for the continuity of the mind and it also is responsible for the afflicted mentality which is responsible for generating the disturbing emotions.

THE IMMEDIATE ASPECT OF THE SEVENTH CONSCIOUSNESS

17. The first of those is immediate because
It is the condition for the arising and ceasing of the six consciousnesses.
It occurs in the same numbers as those of
The momentary arising and ceasing of the six consciousnesses.
It can be known by a mind that is yoga-endowed
And through the teachings of the Victorious One.

The third condition of the four conditions needed for perception to occur is called the immediate condition. When we consider both the afflicted and the immediate mind of the seventh consciousness, we must know that they are always present within the six consciousnesses. The instant a visual object is seen, for example, the visual consciousness ceases, allowing the next instant of consciousness to arise. This sequence applies to all six consciousnesses. The immediate mind is the condition for the immediate arising and cessation of the six consciousnesses; when a consciousness ceases, it does not disappear, instead it subsides into the ground consciousness. The immediate mind is the condition for all appearances to arise from any of the consciousnesses and to settle into the ground consciousness.

How does the immediate mentality cause instants of the mind to arise? An instant of mind cannot arise if there isn't a preceding instant of mind that ceases. There has to be a continuum of instants that immediately follow the preceding instants. When one instant of mind ceases, a latency in the ground consciousness immediately manifests as the next instant of mind. This power of immediacy never declines. It is continually present, so that the continuity of the mind is never interrupted.

How can we know this to be true? This can be seen by the "yoga-endowed." The word *yoga* is Sanskrit for "union" and in this context refers to the union of tranquillity and insight meditation. By directly seeing our mind with shamatha and vipashyana meditation, we can see the immediate mind. We see how the arising of the six consciousness themselves is also a precondition for the arising of the six consciousness—because of the immediate consciousness, an instant of consciousness settles into the ground consciousness as soon as it ceases. The other method of gaining this knowledge is by understanding the Victorious One's (the Buddha's) teachings. We are able to understand that the immediate mind arises on account of there being a condition for the six consciousnesses, and that it is also a condition for their arising.

It has been explained how all phenomena arise from the mind and how the mind itself is empty. With everything in samsara and nirvana appearing from the mind, we discover that the mind itself manifests as the eight consciousnesses. We all experience phenomena differently, for example, two people can go to the same movie and one will love it and the other will hate it. Also beings in the six different realms experience phenomena differently. Hungry ghosts, for example, will perceive all kinds of desirable things and also perceive that they can't obtain them.[31] All experiences whether happiness or suffering, are due to particular causes and conditions. The basic cause of these experiences is the eighth ground consciousness, the *alaya* consciousness. We can begin to understand the function of the ground consciousness through our daily experience. We have a basic clarity of the mind which is an awareness or a continuous knowing. When we look, hear, think, and so on there is always a continuity of the mind; a knowing that accompanies us from birth until death; with the continuum of this clarity present until we achieve Buddhahood. Every action we take creates a latent karmic imprint and these tendencies automatically flow into the ground consciousness where they are stored. These karmic imprints do not, however, remain stored as they manifest sooner or later, which then becomes our experience of samsara.

THE AFFLICTED ASPECT OF THE SEVENTH CONSCIOUSNESS

18. The second is an aspect of this immediate mentality.
It is called the afflicted-mentality because
It believes the mind as self, possesses pride,
Has attachment to the self, and has ignorance,
And gives rise to all the destructive views.

After the six consciousnesses are described, the text commences explaining the seventh consciousness. This consciousness is afflicted and immediate. The seventh consciousness is the ever-present feeling of "I" or "self," the basis of ego. Because the mind is bound by this consciousness, it is called afflicted. The feeling of "I" is present in one instant and when that instant ceases, it is present in the next instant. That is why it is called the immediate consciousness. There is never a discontinuity in the mental continuum; as long as there is a mind, there is a continuous succession of instants immediately proceeding each other. We cannot say that this succession of instants stops even after a hundred years. There is the continuous succession of instants of consciousness and this is called the immediate consciousness.

The seventh (afflicted) consciousness is also present in all beings as a very subtle clinging to a self, which is often explained in terms of mind and mental events.[32] Mind and mental events refer to the clarity and awareness of the mind which sees the nature of things. Mind is the basic awareness and includes all the consciousnesses. When the mind changes, a mental event arises. There are fifty-one mental events[33] listed in the Abhidharma. A mental event denotes that the mind has undergone a change—aspiration gradually becomes *samadhi,* which are positive, and feelings of resentment may become deceit, which are negative.

The afflicted mind is described in term of four mental events: (1) clinging to a self by thinking there is a "me" and "I" (2) pride which is believing the "I" is superior; (3) attachment to the self which is believing oneself more deserving than others; (4) and ignorance which accompanies the above three and is ignoring how things truly are (i.e., the egolessness of self). We may wonder whether the afflicted mind is good or bad. Generally, there are three types of actions or karma: (1) good action or karma, done with the motivation to help others, (2) bad action or karma, done with the motivation to harm others, and (3) neutral action such as walking, eating, or sitting which has neither a good or bad motivation. There are two kinds of neutral actions: those that do not obscure liberation, and those that do. Walking somewhere does not cause obscurations or prevent liberation, whereas clinging to a self does prevent liberation, and so is an obstacle. Yet it is in itself not good or bad, because, if we think something like, "Oh, I must do good actions and need to accumulate merit" subsequent actions are good, or conversely, "Oh, I have to do something bad" the subsequent action is a bad action.

Rangjung Dorje presents a fairly unique view of the seventh consciousness. Generally, those works taught by Buddha in the Mahayana that discuss emptiness are called the sutras and the Buddha's instructions on meditation deities and Vajrayana practice are called the tantras. The teachings given by the Buddha were translated into Tibetan and placed in a collection called the Kangyur. There are two sections to the Kangyur: one dealing with the sutras and one dealing with the tantras. The Third Karmapa used both the sutras and the tantras for this text. His description of how the eighth consciousness stores karmic imprints is clarified in a tantra called *The Tantra of the Vajra's Point* which deals with how the mind manifests external phenomena. In the sutras of the Kangyur the Cittamatrins, in their teaching on the eight consciousnesses, taught the seventh consciousness was only an afflicted consciousness underlying a continuous belief in a self, but was not involved in the immediate condition. Rangjung Dorje's own special view, however, combines this sutra and tantra view and adds the Madhyamaka view to the Cittamatra view, so that the seventh consciousness here is taught to have the aspect of immediate mentality as well as afflicted mentality.

CHARACTERISTICS OF THE IMMEDIATE AND AFFLICTED MENTALITIES

19. The immediate mentality, which is instantaneous
Upon the cessation of the six consciousnesses,
Is the location for the arising of those consciousnesses.
The afflicted mentality is the location for the afflictions.
Therefore, mentality has two aspects
Due to their power to create, and its power to obscure.

Another way to look at mind is to consider it not being a single entity, but being instead a succession of instants. The moment an instant of consciousness arises, it ceases, allowing the next instant of consciousness to arise. Within this progressive succession of instants, external objects are perceived. We may think that the presence of an external object causes sensory consciousnesses to arise, and therefore that an external object is the causal condition, and that the sensory consciousnesses are its effect. However, if an object were the cause, and the consciousness were its result, then what would happen when the instant passed? When there is an effect, where is its cause—the object perceived? The object would have to have ceased to exist, because it was the cause; thus, there is nothing present in terms of an object. If a consciousness were the result in the following instant of consciousness, and its cause had existed in the previous instant, then the consciousness (the effect) would not be present when the object is present (the cause). They would not be connected and, therefore, have no relationship; thus, one cannot be the cause and the other the effect. We may claim that they exist at the same time, in a cause and effect relationship. Yet if they existed simultaneously, there would be no need for a cause, because its effect would already be present. Therefore, it is not logical to claim that an external object is the cause for a sensory consciousness of that object.

Non-Buddhist and Hinayana Buddhists say that the mind and external objects are different, however. If we carefully analyze the situation, we discover that external objects and inner mind are one. External objects actually arise from the mind, just like a dream. In a dream we see forms, but there are no forms that exist outside of our mind. In a dream we see, hear, smell, taste, and feel bodily sensations, but there are no sounds, smells, tastes, or sensations existing outside our mind. Yet they do have appearance; an unreal appearance. Similarly, while waking, everything we see is an appearance, and arises from our mind.

Finally, Rangjung Dorje summaries the two main functions of the afflicted consciousness. The afflicted consciousness is the source or "locations" for the arising negative emotions or afflictions. This continuously present belief in a self gives rise to desire, anger, ignorance, envy, pride, and so on. This verse then concludes that the seventh consciousness has two aspects: the power to create the six consciousnesses (the immediate aspect) and the power to obscure or prevents the attainment of liberation (the afflicted aspect).

THE GROUND CONSCIOUSNESS

20. To those with superior understanding,
The Buddha taught the 'ground consciousness.'
It was also named the 'foundation consciousnesses.'
The 'location consciousness,'
and the 'acquiring consciousness.'
All the actions created by the other seven consciousnesses
Are accumulated, distinctly and impartially within it,
Like rain and rivers flowing into the ocean.
Therefore it is also named the 'ripening consciousness.'

The first two levels of this verse is a brief explanation of the eighth (ground) consciousness and the rest of the lines are the detailed description of this consciousness.

The fourth of the four conditions for perception to occur is the causal condition, or the ground consciousness. The ground or *alaya* consciousness was not mentioned in the Theravada texts which describe only the first six consciousnesses. The seventh and eighth consciousnesses were not taught in the Buddha's early teachings because it could have easily have incorrectly been taken for being permanent and unique and therefore the same as a permanent self (Skt. *atman*). However, the ground consciousness is not a permanent self because its nature is emptiness and it is the source of all samsaric appearances. A self is considered very important and we have great attachment to it, but this isn't true for the ground consciousness. In the Abhidharma teachings, however, the Buddha said, "I have explained the ground consciousness to those who are pure," meaning that the ground consciousness was introduced to Mahayana bodhisattvas who are called "those with superior understanding" in this verse.

The ground consciousness has many functions so Rangjung Dorje explains these by giving each of them names. It is called the "basis consciousness" because the eighth consciousness is the basis for the mind; it is called the "location consciousness" because it is the location of the mind, and it is called the "acquisition consciousness" because it acquires all the karmic latencies that are laid down.

The reason the Buddha taught the subject of the ground consciousness at all is that when karma accumulates, the latent karmic imprints settle in the ground consciousness to express themselves at a later time. A karmic latency will awaken as experiences of suffering or happiness. Positive karma[34] doesn't immediately express itself as happiness; so doing many positive deeds will not result in a rebirth in a paradise. Rather the karmic latencies rest within the ground consciousness and arise later as a result, for example, joy for being reborn in a slightly higher situation. Similarly, accumulated negative karma does not express itself immediately as rebirth in the hell realms, but the karmic imprints remain in the ground consciousness to ripen under the appropriate circumstances causing suffering later on. Thus the ground consciousness can be said to be the "ripening consciousness."

The negative emotions and the positive qualities increase and grow due to habituation. For example, a person becomes angry again and again and then becomes habituated to anger, causing the latency of anger increases in the mind. The same is true with desire. When one desires something again and again, the latencies of desire increase. This process also occurs for the positive qualities: a person may not have much love, compassion, or wisdom, but by engaging in love, compassion, or study; the imprints of these positive qualities increase in the ground consciousness. If there were only six consciousnesses, then thoughts would arise and cease without anything left to increase or develop such as the good qualities to reach Buddhahood. The increase of these positive qualities occurs only because positive tendencies are planted in the ground consciousness.

The ground consciousness is the foundation and location for the mind because all karmic latencies are stored in the ground consciousness. A momentary visual consciousness instantly ceases (when the next instant appears) and does not occur again; instead a new momentary visual consciousness appears. Similarly, a mental consciousness is created and ceases instantly; sometimes a mental consciousness does not appear at all. However, the latencies for the arising of these consciousnesses are contained within the ground consciousness. Thus, we can remember a visual perception that occurred in the past; and remembering it, strengthens the latency.

The ground consciousness is very important for our practice of the Dharma. If we do not maintain mindfulness and awareness, our disturbing emotions gradually increase, from day to day, from lifetime to lifetime. However, if we develop mindfulness and awareness, our mind will gradually improve due to the latencies being established in the ground consciousness. For example, when we begin to practice, there may not be much love and compassion in our meditation. But if we persist and meditate on love and compassion, through the gradual accumulation of the latencies of love and compassion in the ground consciousness, we will gradually progress to a point where our meditation will have vast love and compassion.

In terms of Dharma practice, the ground consciousness is very important, because through meditation our mind overcomes negativity and develops positive imprints. Habituating ourselves to positive thoughts and actions allows negative imprints to decrease and positive qualities to increase. Meditation is very similar to habituation.[35] By developing samadhi, negative tendencies transform into positive imprints, which can be developed until Buddhahood is attained.

We can witness the effect of latencies in our daily life. Some children are very intelligent and some are not. This is due to the presence or absence of latencies to study in previous lifetimes. Some children are naturally very kind due to positive latencies laid down in their ground consciousnesses in previous lifetimes, and some children are very aggressive, due to negative latencies. We can also see an aggressive child who has bad behavior gradually changes as he grows older; through his cultivation of mindfulness and awareness, he can slowly with the right training establish new latencies by developing love, compassion, and humility as an adult. Conversely some good children grow up to be bad due to the negative latencies they establish during their childhood.

The eighth consciousness is also the foundation of experience. Should someone be born into a higher existence as a god, jealous god, or human being his or her experiences of happiness would be based upon the ground consciousness, and should someone fall into the lower realms, his or her experiences would also be based on the ground consciousness. Thus the eighth consciousness is the basis of all experiences within samsara, including future experiences. Creating imprints in the present leads to experiencing their results in the future; like a child who goes to school and studies hard—that activity will create an imprint in the child's mind that will allow him or her to become a teacher later on. If there were not learning, there would be no imprint, and no possibility of being a teacher in the future. This is how the eighth consciousness functions and why it is responsible for the various existences in samsara, and why it is also called the consciousness of acquisition.

The five sensory and the sixth mental consciousness are either positive, negative, or neutral. The seventh (afflicted) consciousness is neutral but has two possibilities: it may be ignorant and therefore the basis of the disturbing emotions, and may be obscuring because it obscures liberation. The eight (ground) consciousness is also neutral; however, it is not obscuring like the afflicted consciousness, it instead has an aspect of clarity. This clarity allows all phenomena (places, bodies, existences, and so forth) to manifest, but does not obscure liberation.

The other seven consciousnesses create positive and negative imprints in the eighth consciousness. A simile to how this occurs is given in the text: when it rains, the water naturally flows into the rivers, and the rivers, whether they are dirty or clean, naturally flow into the ocean. Similarly, positive and negative imprints naturally flow into the ground consciousness.

21. As it creates everything,
And is the ground from which all seeds sprout,
It is described as 'the causal condition'.
However, because it is eliminated
When the seven consciousnesses are negated.
It is also called the 'conditional consciousness.'

All the karmic seeds, good or bad, within the ground consciousness, sprout and manifest as the other seven consciousnesses, as if the ground-consciousness were the ocean and the other seven consciousnesses were waves that appear upon its surface. The ground consciousness is responsible for all illusory appearances, but is not the basis of Buddhahood, which is freedom from delusion. This is why the eighth consciousness is a consciousness and not a wisdom.

This concludes the section of the treatise that deals with the impure states of mind, the consciousnesses. The ground consciousness is the source of all delusory experiences. It is not the basis of Buddhahood because Buddhahood is freedom from delusion. The nature of the ground consciousness is delusion; it is not in harmony with the true nature of reality. When Buddhahood or *arhatship* is attained, the ground consciousness continues to exists. When the ground consciousness ceases, all the consciousnesses are transformed into ultimate wisdom.

To summarize there are impure consciousnesses and pure wisdom. In defining the impure consciousnesses it has been taught that the root of samsara and nirvana is the mind and that the mind itself is birthless.

Table 4

Transformation of the Consciousnesses into Wisdoms

Realm	Consciousness	Wisdom
Dharmakaya	8th consciousness	Mirror-like-Wisdom
Sambhogakaya	7th (klesha aspect)	Wisdom of Equality
	7th (immediate aspect)	Discriminating Wisdom
Nirmanakaya	5 sensory consciousnesses and nonconceptual 6th	All-Accomplishing Wisdom
	6th mental consciousness	Dharmadhatu wisdom

PART II

The Five Wisdoms

Table 5
The Five Paths

1. Path of Accumulation	Practices mindfulness, Recognizes the four marks of existence (impermanence, absence of a self, suffering, and emptiness). practices four renunciations, four practices of concentrative Absorption (strong interest, perseverance, inattentiveness, and investigation)
2. Path of Application	Five controlling powers (confidence, sustained effort,
mindfulness,	samadhi, and prajna). These powers become "unshakable" at the end of this path.
3. Path of Insight	One attains the first bodhisattva level of perceiving emptiness. Develops true awareness of the Four Noble Truths and their 16 aspects. Develops the seven factors of enlightenment (memory, investigation of meaning and values, effort, joy, refinement and serenity, samadhi, equanimity).
4. Path of Cultivation (Meditation)	One goes through the 2nd to 10th bodhisattva levels. One practices the eight-fold Noble Path (right view, right intention, right speech, right action, right livelihood, right effort, right, and right meditation).
5. Path of Fulfillment	This is Buddhahood.

Chapter 5

The Transformation of the Consciousnesses into the Wisdoms

THE FIVE WISDOMS AND THE THREE KAYAS

Jamgon Kongtrul has written a commentary on this text called *The Adornment of Rangjung Dorje's View.* At this point Jamgon Kongtrul has added information on how the five aggregates (Skt. *skandhas*) are transformed into wisdoms at the time of Buddhahood. Although this does not appear in Rangjung Dorje's treatise, it will be helpful to discuss it here.

The five aggregates literally mean "heaps" and are form, sensation, perception, formation, and consciousness. Each of these aggregates is transformed upon reaching enlightenment. The aggregate of sensation (which includes within itself the three kinds of suffering: the suffering of suffering, the suffering of change, and the all-pervasive suffering) transforms into freedom from suffering, as well as an unbroken continuity of great bliss. The aggregate of perception is transformed into the unhindered ability to teach the Dharma. The aggregate of formation is transformed into miraculous deeds, and the gathering of dharma students. Finally, the aggregates of consciousnesses are transformed into the five wisdoms. As may be seen it is the sixth mental consciousness which is the aspect of mind that becomes the wisdoms at the level of enlightenment.

Jamgon Kongtrul describes four causes within the practice of the path of Dharma which give rise to four of the five wisdoms. Hearing and contemplating the full range of the Buddha's teachings in the Tripitaka (the Vinaya, the Sutras and the Abhidharma) will cause 'mirror-like wisdom' to develop. Engaging in the meditation of helping all sentient beings without any partiality to friends or aversion to enemies will cause the 'wisdom of equality.' The giving of Dharma teachings with the motivation of love and compassion and a desire to help all sentient beings will cause 'discriminating wisdom' to develop. Finally, the accomplishing of activities to benefit others is the cause for 'all-accomplishing wisdom'. We could add that the realization of the true nature of phenomena is the cause for the fifth 'dharmadhatu wisdom'.

There are three realms (Skt. *kayas*). These are the dharmakaya, which is the pure realm of complete enlightenment. This manifests as the sambhogakaya which is a pure realm where only realized beings (bodhisattvas and buddhas) can visit and receive teachings. Finally, there is the nirmanakaya, which is our earthly realm inhabited by beings in samsara.

By diligently listening to and contemplating the Dharma and meditating on it, we are able to slowly eliminate the afflictions and gradually develop the wisdom of the true nature of phenomena. We progress through the ten bodhisattva levels terminating in the attainment of Buddhahood. At this point we have completely eliminated the causes of samsara, negative karma, and the disturbing emotions. Our suffering is replaced with the experience of great bliss and peace. This is the first benefit of Buddhahood, which principally liberates oneself. Upon attaining Buddhahood we also eliminate all obstacles to our wisdom and attain perfect realization or "omniscience." This benefits others because with this knowledge we can show them how they too can attain Buddhahood. This complete elimination of the disturbing emotions and the cognitive obstructions is the Buddha's 'dharmakaya' or "the body of the dharma." This elimination of emotional and cognitive obstacles is illustrated by the Tibetan name for the "Buddha" which is *sang gye*. The first syllable *sang* denotes the Buddha has eliminated all defilements and the second syllable *gye* denotes the Buddha has full realization.

The dharmakaya is principally an emanation of the Buddha's mind and has three qualities to help sentient beings. The dharmakaya has the quality of complete wisdom; it manifests compassion for all beings, and the power to provide refuge for them.

The dharmakaya is divided into two kayas or bodies: the dharmakaya and the svabhavikakaya. The aspect of the dharmakaya which is the wisdom of the variety of phenomena (Tib. *ji nye pa*) is called the 'dharmakaya'. The aspect of the dharmakaya which is the wisdom of the true nature of phenomena (Tib. *ji ta ba*) is the "svabhavikakaya." Under this system the realms become four.

The clarity of the dharmakaya's wisdom is called 'the mirror-like wisdom'. All images whether a king's castle or rotting meat appear clearly as in a mirror. But while clearly seen, there is no attachment to these appearances. The Buddha is able to clearly see human being's purity and impurities, their delusions and suffering. Due to mirror-like wisdom everything is precisely known by the Buddha. Whatever is reflected in the mirror of this wisdom appears unmistakably, that is, white does not appear as yellow or yellow does not appear as red. Similarly, the dharmakaya perceives everything as it really is.

The sambhogakaya comes from the Sanskrit word *kaya* which literally means "body" and *sambhoga* meaning "enjoyment." The Sanskrit word refers to the spreading of Buddha's activity among those interested in receiving teachings. Usually, enjoyment has another connotation of receiving wealth and pleasure, but that is not the enjoyment of a buddha. Enjoyment in this context refers to buddha activity bringing all bodhisattvas to the state of Buddhahood. Through the Buddha's activity, the bodhisattvas are endowed with enjoyment. The sambhogakaya has two wisdoms: firstly, the wisdom of equanimity, in which everything is seen impartially. With this wisdom there is no differentiation between important and unimportant, self and other, best or worst; nevertheless, this does not mean that a buddha cannot discern good and bad, suffering and bliss, delusion and non-delusion. The sambhogakaya can discriminate between these because the sambhogakaya has the second wisdom; discriminating awareness—phenomena are distinguished accurately, but are viewed impartially.

Impure beings that have no aspiration to receive Dharma teachings and have various dispositions and interests also exist. That is why buddhas manifest in different ways. In the sutras it is written that some persons enter the path by encountering a buddha's body, a buddha in a *form body*. Some persons enter the path upon hearing a buddha's teachings such as Shakyamuni's student Shariputra who completely understood his teachings by just hearing them. Others enter the path upon seeing miracles; so the Buddha sent persons like Maudgalyana[36] to perform miracles. Yet others enter the path by observing the Buddha's behavior, such as Shakyamuni's pupil Upali who was impressed by the Buddha's perfect behavior of dressing properly, walking with discipline, and so on. The nirmanakaya also has the wisdom of all-accomplishing actions.

The Buddha, being completely free of delusion, can correctly teach other beings, and free them from delusions so that they also will be able to see the true nature of things. The wisdom that sees the true nature of phenomena is the dharmadhatu wisdom and belongs to the svabhavikakaya.

THE TRANSFORMATION OF THE GROUND CONSCIOUSNESS[37]

22. This ground consciousness,
Which is the identity of everything external and internal,
Is the source of everything that should be eliminated.
It has been taught that it will be overcome
By the 'vajra-samadhi'.

We now return to the root text that begins this second section on the five wisdoms with an explanation of the transformation of the ground consciousness into the five wisdoms.

As mentioned before Rangjung Dorje uses a mahamudra view of the ground consciousness which is a little different from how it is traditionally presented by the Cittamatrins who held that the ground consciousness is truly existent and the source of samsara and nirvana. If the ground consciousness were the source of nirvana, then we would have to conclude that the ground consciousness continues after the attainment of Buddhahood. However, in this treatise the ground consciousness is said to be completely empty and the foundation from which all the delusions of samsara appear, that is, as the storehouse containing all the latencies of samsaric appearance. Although its nature is neutral, and it does not impede liberation in itself, it is the source of everything that has to be eliminated. This suggests that the ground consciousness is the foundation for samsara, but not for nirvana. When the ground consciousness is eliminated by "the vajra samadhi" with *vajra* meaning something which is "indestructible" and *samadhi* meaning "meditation," it is transformed into the wisdoms and is no longer the ground consciousness. So the nature of the ground consciousness is delusion; not the true nature of reality. When Buddhahood or *arhatship* is attained, the ground consciousness ends.

The ground consciousness is the true identity of external phenomena such as mountains and the internal phenomena such as thoughts. This is because the ground consciousness is the source of all the illusory appearances of samsara. Although its nature is neutral, and it does not impede liberation in itself, it is the source of everything that has to be eliminated.

MIRROR-LIKE WISDOM[38]

23. When the ground consciousness, with its obscurations,
is negated
At that time, there will be the 'mirror wisdom'.
All wisdoms appear in it, without the concept of "mine."
It is uncircumscribed and eternally possessed.
It realizes all that is to be known,
without being directed towards them.
It is described as 'the dharmakaya,'
Because it is the foundation for all the wisdoms.

The first wisdom is the mirror-like wisdom, which is the wisdom of the dharmakaya. The eight consciousnesses are transformed into the five wisdoms when a person is about to become a buddha. At this boundary, there is a final trace of the ground consciousness left that is eliminated by the vajra-like samadhi and Buddhahood is achieved, transforming the ground consciousness into mirror-like wisdom.

Since mirror-like wisdom itself is freedom from delusions, it sees the delusions, experiences, aspirations and interests of others as clearly as if they were reflected in a mirror. Ordinarily, we can see only what is in front of us, but mirror-like wisdom enables us to see everything in all directions, without any mistakes at all and it leads to great understanding because all aspects are seen so clearly.

From the clarity or luminosity of the ground consciousness, external phenomena seem to be really there, as if they were external objects. The ground consciousness also gives rise to internal phenomena of our mind being seen as the self, resulting in the development of the mind poisons, such as attachment and anger. All these phenomena that come from the ground consciousness appear very vividly to us. When the ground consciousness has been transformed into mirror-like wisdom, there aren't any more clear or vivid delusions or appearances of samsara: clarity becomes this mirror-like wisdom. We may wonder if the elimination of the ground consciousness results in an emptiness such as a vacuum of empty space. But since it isn't like that, this state is described as a mirror in which a reflection appears vividly, without any sense of self. There is no grasping at the thought of "I" or "me," everything just appears clearly.

A wisdom may be permanent or changing. For example, the wisdom of all-accomplishing actions undergoes changes depending on the needs of sentient beings, whereas the mirror-like wisdom is changeless, continuously present, and permanent like the ground consciousness. Anything, whether beneficial or harmful, will appear to the mirror-like wisdom clearly, continuously, and impartially without any distinction between self and other.

Mirror-like wisdom is the wisdom of love and compassion; it gives rise to compassion, and that compassion gives rise to power. Unlike the ground consciousness, which is the root of all the illusory appearances of samsara, mirror-like wisdom is the source of the five wisdoms and is called the dharmakaya (Tib. *chö kyi ku*). The Sanskrit word *kaya* means "body" or "aspect" and the word *Dharma* comes from *dru dhrina,* meaning "to hold," thus, Dharma means to hold something, so it doesn't fall down. So Dharma means things are prevented from falling down into samsara or lower existences. The word *Dharma* was translated into Tibetan as *chö* which means "to repair, correct, or heal." For example, if an error were to occur, we would correct it; the Tibetan word for correcting something is *chö.* It is also used to heal an illness, and to describe situations where everything is going well or prospering—where all the good qualities are being developed and all the negative things are being eliminated.

THE WISDOM OF EQUALITY

24. The 'afflicted mentality'
Is utterly defeated by the 'fearless samadhi.'
The kleshas are utterly eliminated on
the paths of insight and meditation.
The subsequent absence of afflictions,

The absence of samsara and nirvana,
Is described as the 'wisdom of equality.'

The second wisdom is the wisdom of equality or equanimity, which is the result of the seventh (afflicted) consciousness having been transformed. The afflicted consciousness possesses subtle ego-clinging until it is transformed, and there is no longer a distinction between self and other or the thought of "I" and "mine." This transformation occurs at the eighth bodhisattva level, and is attained through the samadhi of fearlessness, whose courage is compared to that of a lion—an animal that cannot be defeated by any of the other animals.

This courageous samadhi or meditation overcomes the afflicted mentality of the seventh consciousness. When we are thus afflicted by clinging to a belief in a self, everything becomes frightening and we become cowards. Even if a little stone is flicked at us we instinctively react in fear. This is because we are clinging to a self, and are afraid of the self being harmed. The courageous meditation enables us to overcome the afflicted mentality, and not be afraid of anything or anyone.

Until the eighth bodhisattva level we engage in samadhi which still has some disturbing emotions or kleshas present. Sometimes the samadhi is stable; at other times the disturbing emotions arise and must be eliminated. In any case, they are completely pacified on the eighth bodhisattva level.

Different kinds of disturbing emotions are eliminated on the five paths of meditation. On the first two paths, those of accumulation and junction, disturbing emotions become controlled and overcome, but their seeds are still present. Consequently, this second path is one of aspiration—the aspiration to eliminate the disturbing emotions. On the third path, that of insight, the true nature of phenomena is realized but it is not enough to eradicate the poisons because we need to become familiarized with prevailing insight, and meditate to intensify the tendency of seeing the true nature of phenomena. On the fourth path, that of meditation, we habituate ourselves to that insight.

The obvious and coarse disturbing emotions are vanquished when the true nature of phenomena is first seen. The subtle disturbing emotions, however, are not eliminated until the path of meditation. For example, when we see something special, attachment and craving arise, when they have been eliminated, everything is seen impartially, with an understanding of the equality of all things. This also applies to anger, because anger implies things are unpleasant, and to aggression; when they are eliminated, everything is seen impartially. Similarly, pride creates a biased opinion; when it is eliminated, all beings are considered impartially. Ignorance is partial understanding, and is of two types—mixed and unmixed. Mixed ignorance arises with desire, anger, and pride; when it is eliminated, everything is understood equally, and a state of equality and peace are established.

There is the gradual elimination of the disturbing emotions beginning on the path of vision and lasting throughout the path of meditation. The disturbing emotions gradually decrease and the wisdoms gradually increase. When the afflicted consciousness is completely vanquished on the eighth bodhisattva level, then the last disturbing emotion ends and the complete wisdom of equality is attained.

Not only is the afflicted mentality eliminated, but also the disturbing emotions or afflictions are eliminated by the third and fourth paths: the path of insight and the path of meditation, which correspond to the tenth bodhisattva level. The conceptual aspects of the afflicted consciousness is eliminated by seeing the true nature of phenomena, while the subtle, inherent aspects are eliminated by meditation.

While there are disturbing emotions and attachment to a self, there is a division into good and bad, self and other, resulting in many different kinds of suffering; one thinks oneself better than others, so there is pride or one thinks that others are doing better than oneself, resulting in envy and jealousy.

When the afflictions are eliminated, the wisdom of equality is attained. It is named the wisdom of equality because everything appears equally good and pure to it, with no differentiation of good or bad, enemies or friends.

DISCRIMINATING WISDOM: THE PURIFIER AND PURIFIED

25. The immediate mentality
Is called 'the sustainer', because it sustains the six consciousnesses.
It is called 'thought', because it gives rise to thoughts.
It is defeated by true understanding and the 'illusion-samadhi'.

The seventh consciousness has two aspects: the afflicted and the immediate mind. As previously mentioned, the afflicted mind transforms into the wisdom of equality at the eighth bodhisattva level; however, the immediate mind, along with the sixth mental consciousness, transforms into discriminating wisdom at enlightenment.

Discriminating wisdom relates to the five sensory consciousnesses and the sixth mental consciousness. Discrimination of experiences is due to the six consciousnesses, whether the experience arises from one of the five senses or from the mental consciousness. This wisdom knows each thing just as it is and therefore is called "discriminating wisdom" because all experiences of the six consciousnesses are clearly seen.

The first five sensory consciousnesses nonconceptually perceive whatever clearly appears—one thing not seen as many, and many things are not seen as one. Conversely, the sixth consciousness conceives one thing as many, and many as one. For example, a visual consciousness perceives a conch shell as a single object, whereas the mental consciousness conceives its color, shape and so on. Externally, the conch is one object, but it becomes many objects in the mind. Also, many things can be perceived as one. A visual consciousness perceives a big and a little conch as separate objects whereas the mental consciousness, thinks that all conches are one—the little conch on the shrine, the big one behind the door, another one on the table—all are seen as conches. When the seventh immediate consciousness is transformed into discriminating wisdom, it perceives different qualities clearly, and understanding or discrimination of various things develops. When does this transformation occur? As previously explained, mirror-like wisdom is attained through the vajra-like samadhi; the wisdom of equality is attained through the fearless samadhi, and discriminating wisdom is achieved through the samadhi that knows everything to be an illusion. That knowing signifies the understanding of emptiness that is achieved on the first bodhisattva level of perfect joy. One can also say it is established on the third path of insight, because of the understanding achieved on the first two paths. The second path, of junction consists of four stages: the stage of warmth, patience, peak, and supreme Dharma. Discriminating wisdom begins developing on the sixth bodhisattva level, that of great patience. It is achieved on the third path, that of insight, and is completely perfected on the eighth bodhisattva level. Bodhisattvas, having attained perfect discriminating wisdom on the eighth bodhisattva level, can manifest pure realms to those capable of perceiving them. On the ninth bodhisattva level, great wisdom is achieved, and on the tenth bodhisattva level, the bodhisattva possesses the same activity as a Buddha. The qualities of the eighth, ninth, and tenth bodhisattva levels are due to discriminating wisdom.

The essence of the sixth (mental) consciousness is that it grasps things as good or bad resulting in a constant state of delusion. When this delusion has been transformed, mental fixation stops, resulting in the correct understanding that is discriminating wisdom. With discriminating wisdom, all the obscurations are removed, and one sees things just as they are. With the wisdom of equality, one sees the sameness of all phenomena, and could make mistakes, but don't. Because of discriminating wisdom, a Buddha doesn't ever make mistakes in time. The above process is overcome by illusionary samadhi that occurs with the state of great equanimity, attained at the eighth bodhisattva level.

The immediate mentality is a continuum that causes the arising and cessation of the six sensory consciousnesses, thus sustaining the six consciousnesses, and is therefore known as "the sustainer." Since it also gives rise to thoughts, it is also called "thought." As these thoughts can only be deluded, since the true nature is not realized, they can be eliminated only by true understanding and by the illusion-samadhi. True understanding realizes the impermanence, suffering, and the emptiness of phenomena. The illusion-samadhi has the knowledge that the mind and its objects are all illusions, therefore realization of emptiness arises.

DISCRIMINATING WISDOM: THE RESULT OF PURIFICATION

25b. When 'the great patience' is attained.
Due to the transformation of precepts and perceiver
There is a manifestation of pure realms,
The wisdom of all times,
And total, unimpeded activity.
The thoughts involved in these, transformed
Become 'discriminating wisdom'.

The "great patience," sometimes called the "great equanimity" is the complete and thorough achievement of the paramita of patience and this is attained at the eighth bodhisattva level, which is called the unshakable level. At this stage, the perceiver and precepts are transformed so that one can actually enter into the *pure realm* and can also manifest pure realms to others. At the ninth bodhisattva level, the thoughts of the eighth level transform into unimpeded wisdom of all times, meaning one has the wisdom of the past, present, and future. Finally, at the tenth bodhisattva level, thoughts transform into an unimpeded engagement with all the various kinds of activity required to train beings. The ultimate transformation of all such thoughts into the discriminating wisdom occurs at the level of Buddhahood which some systems place at the tenth level and others at the thirteen level.[39] It is discriminating wisdom knowing all that is to be known, exactly as they are, distinctly and individually.

To summarize, ground consciousness is transformed into the mirror-like wisdom and the afflicted consciousness into the wisdom of equality. The sambhogakaya possesses two wisdoms: the wisdom of equality and the discriminating wisdom. The immediate consciousness is transformed into discriminating wisdom.

THE SAMBHOGAKAYA

26. These two wisdoms of equality and discrimination are
Pure meditation, through which there
no abiding in samsara and nirvana
The possession of peace, love, and compassion;
The manifestation of various bodies;
And teachings to the retinues.
The mandala of the melody of the great Dharma is manifest

And a treasury of all samadhis and dharanis
This is named the sambhogakaya.

After the dharmakaya, which is the realm of complete unimpeded truth, has been described, the sambhogakaya in relation to the wisdom is described. The Sanskrit word, sambhogakaya, literally means the body of perfect or complete enjoyment, and was translated into Tibetan as *long chö dzok ku. Long chö* means "enjoyment" or "pleasures," *dzok pa* means "complete," and *ku* means "body." To understand this word we must ask, "What pleasures does a buddha have?" The sambhogakaya form of the buddha teaches the Dharma to bodhisattvas who have already transcended suffering by attaining the bodhisattva levels. A buddha has the happiness of thinking that he or she has been able to benefit these beings, and is not worried that he or she will slide back into suffering. The activity of a buddha is perfected in the sambhogakaya, in which a buddha is able to present the perfect wisdom, meditation, and activity to bodhisattvas. Therefore, all the pleasures of the Dharma derive from the sambhogakaya.

The essence of the sambhogakaya is the wisdom of equality and the wisdom of discrimination. The wisdom of equality allows the buddhas to see all sentient beings without prejudice, without thinking, "this being is more worthy of enlightenment than that being;" so this wisdom gives rise to great compassion. The second discriminating wisdom allows the buddhas to see everything as it actually is, completely and without any mistakes, so they can engage in flawless buddha activity. We can contrast the sambhogakaya with the nirmanakaya, which is the realm we live in presently. Here the buddhas manifest as living beings in five ways.

In the sambhogakaya there are: (1) a definite retinue that is entirely made up of bodhisattvas residing in the ten bodhisattva levels. In the nirmanakaya the buddha is surrounded by more or less diligent pupils, by persons with or without devotion, and by the faithful and the faithless; (2) a definite place which is the pure realm. A nirmanakaya buddha sometimes manifests in a pure realm, and sometimes in an impure realm, whereas a sambhogakaya buddha can only be encountered in a pure realm; (3) a definite time, which is continuous. There is a special time a nirmanakaya buddha and his teachings are presented to the world, whereas a sambhogakaya

Buddha is present until samsara ends, and his teachings continue without interruption; (4) the quality of the teachings are exclusively the Mahayana Dharma. A nirmanakaya buddha has pupils at different levels of understanding and introduces them to the Dharma by teaching the definitive teachings to some and the *provisional teachings* to others, whereas the sambhogakaya buddha teaches only the *definitive teachings* of the Mahayana, and (5) a definite teacher is a sambhogakaya buddha. The nirmanakaya buddha possesses the special features of a buddha, and has the appearance of being made of flesh and bones, but his body is not composed of physical substance. Whereas, the sambhogakaya buddha has a completely pure body possessing all the distinctive physical characteristics and this is his definite body.

These two wisdoms of the sambhogakaya arise from pure meditation which is beyond samsara and nirvana. The wisdom of equality leads to a great peace and love and compassion for others. The wisdom of discrimination leads to the manifestation of the sambhogakaya deities who reside in the pure realms, for example, Amitabha who resides in the pure realm of Tushita. In these pure realms, it is said, one hears the continuous teachings of the Dharma, or as the verse says, "the great Dharma melody" which is in the mandala of the pure realm. What is in the mandala of the pure realm? They are all the teachings of the samadhis (meditation) and the dharani (the esoteric part of the Dharma).

THE ALL-ACCOMPLISHING WISDOM

27. The transformation of the five sensory consciousnesses
And the aspect of the mental consciousness directed towards them:
The sixteen wisdoms of the 'patience for knowledge'
And the aspects of the four truths,
That have arisen from correct thought,
See and truly realize the meaning.

The all-accomplishing wisdom is associated with accomplishing all the goals of the Dharma particularly hindrances such as illness and other material obstacles.

The path or map to enlightenment may be described in several ways—as done previously—in terms of the ten bodhisattva levels and in terms of the five paths. The five paths are the path of accumulation, in which we accumulate vast merit and wisdom; the path of junction, in which we are preparing to realize egolessness; the path of insight in which egolessness is first truly realized and is the beginning of the ten bodhisattva levels; the path of meditation in which we develop extremely precise and refined meditation; and the path of no more learning which is the final path.

The Pramana states that the mental consciousness has two aspects: conceptual and nonconceptual. The five sensory consciousnesses and the nonconceptual aspect of the sixth (mental) consciousness, which are impure, are transformed into wisdom through correct examination. Correct examination that has the aspiration for true meditation takes place on the second path, that of juncture. Meditating with that concept of aspiration gives rise to wisdom of the third path, that of insight, and that wisdom sees the nature of the Four Noble Truths: the truth of suffering, the truth of origination, the truth of cessation, and the truth of the path. These truths have two aspects: samsara and nirvana, each of which has a cause and a result. The result of samsara is suffering: this is the first noble truth. The cause of samsara is the kleshas and karma; this is the truth of origination. When the kleshas and karma are eliminated, the result is a state of peace and liberation—nirvana: this is the third noble truth. The cause of nirvana is the application of the method: this is the fourth noble truth.

Each of the Four Noble Truths has four aspects: (1) having no true understanding, but the patience to develop understand, (2) having actual understanding, (3) understanding the attainment more thoroughly at the first bodhisattva level, (4) attaining complete liberation by having eliminated the mental poisons. These four aspects times the four Noble Truths are called the sixteen aspects of liberation on the third path, that of insight, and result in all-accomplishing wisdom.

For example, for the first noble truth of suffering has (1) the obscuration of the nature of suffering, the elimination of which results in the equanimity that understands the nature of suffering, (2) having eliminated that aspect, the nature of suffering is seen resulting in the knowledge of suffering, (3) the outcome of attaining the first two aspect of equanimity of a subsequent understanding of suffering, and (4) the outcome of attaining all three aspects is the subsequent knowledge of the nature of suffering.

When this first noble truth is seen and we "truly realize the meaning," the elimination of all these obstructions to this truth of suffering is called "the patience for the knowledge of the phenomena of suffering."

28. The five sensory consciousnesses are transformed when:
There is an engagement with all sensory objects,
And the power and possession of the twelve qualities
Of all the bodhisattva levels hundred-fold.
When this is developed to the fullest extent,
It becomes the wisdom of accomplishment.

Our senses and their corresponding consciousnesses are very limited. For example, when we are inside a room, our senses can tell us what is going on in the room, but not what is going on outside the room. Also when we look at an individual we don't know what that individual's wishes and desires are. However, upon reaching the third path, that of insight, our senses and their corresponding consciousnesses are transformed into all-accomplishing wisdom. When this wisdom is attained, we can see the true nature of phenomena and we can see the nature of other beings; seeing their state of mind, their aspirations, their capabilities, and also seeing what activity is necessary to teach them.

This wisdom is attained on the first bodhisattva level that is called the level of complete joy. At this point one attains twelve qualities and each quality is in a number of a hundred. Some of these twelve qualities are: seeing a hundred buddhas in one instant; receiving the teachings of a hundred buddhas in one instant; manifesting a hundred emanations in one instant, and so on. At the second bodhisattva level, these twelve qualities increase to a thousand-fold; at the third level, they are a hundred thousand-fold and so on, with their power and benefit increasing until, at the level of Buddhahood, they become the wisdom of accomplishment. This wisdom is attained at the first bodhisattva level, but it is not complete because the wisdom of accomplishment is with the nirmanakaya form of buddha. So this nirmanakaya is not obtained until the complete state of Buddhahood. With the wisdom of accomplishment, a buddha knows completely the true nature of phenomena, the nature of his pupils and the necessary methods required, and so he can effortlessly accomplish benefit for beings.

THE FOUR TYPES OF NIRMANAKAYA

29. This wisdom accomplishes benefit for all beings
Through an incalculable, inconceivable,
variety of emanations through all realms.
This is the Great Nirmanakaya.

Although the twelve deeds are the principal means by which the supreme nirmanakaya leads beings into the Dharma, the Buddha knew through his clairvoyance what specific individuals needed. Some needed to witness miracles to develop faith and enter the Dharma, therefore the Buddha sent Maudgalyana, one of his principal pupils, to display miracles for them. There were others who were not convinced by miracles but were convinced by logic and reasoning, so he sent Shariputra, who excelled in wisdom, to teach them. Those who were not convinced by either miracles or wisdom, but by excellent restrained conduct, were sent Upali, a monk with excellent conduct who inspired faith in them. Some would benefit from the Dharma being taught to them, so the Buddha himself would come to lead them into the Dharma. If persons couldn't be brought into the Dharma by the various methods of the supreme nirmanakaya, the Buddha was able to use the created nirmanakaya, which is instantly created for a certain situation, unlike the supreme nirmanakaya that has first to be born, practice meditation, and achieve Buddhahood through the path.

The wisdom of accomplishment is the wisdom that accomplishes Buddha activity. The supreme nirmanakaya Buddha accomplished the twelve deeds of the world was performed through the wisdom of accomplishment. The reason this wisdom is called the wisdom of accomplishment of activity is that whatever needs to be done, can be done. This can only be done after all the ignorance of the five sensory consciousnesses have been transformed. But now whatever needs to be done to benefit oneself or others can be done without any error or mistake because there is the understanding of all things or omniscience.

There are four different kinds of nirmanakaya manifestations: the supreme nirmanakaya, the created nirmanakaya, the born nirmanakaya, and the various nirmanakaya.

The supreme nirmanakaya is, for example, the Buddha Shakyamuni, who appeared in the world and performed the activities that are summarized in the twelve deeds of the Buddha. The Buddha was in the Tushita pure realm before he entered the womb of his mother and took birth in our world to help all beings. He was born in a grove in Lumbini, Nepal, and later accepted his father's kingdom by becoming a prince, marrying a princess, and having a child. He could just as well have descended from Tushita and been born in a flower (as was Padmasambhava) but there is a reason that he did not. If he had been miraculously born, people would have thought, "It is possible for him to achieve enlightenment because he was miraculously born, whereas I am born of an ordinary mother, and therefore cannot achieve enlightenment." If he had not been a prince, and had not married, people would have thought, "Being an ascetic is different. I am incapable of becoming ordained and leading a wandering life." However, the Buddha in his nirmanakaya form was born in Lumbini, reached Buddhahood at Bodhgaya, and gave Dharma teachings at Varanasi. He taught particular beings with particular actions, until he passed into nirvana.

The second kind of nirmanakaya, the created nirmanakaya, is not born of parents but instead manifests for particular beneficial situations. An example of the created nirmanakaya is a story of Prananda, the king of the *gandharvas* who are the celestial musicians. He played the vina which is an Indian lute. One day Indra, the king of deities, came to him and said, "The Buddha is in the world now and is giving Dharma teachings. Let's go." Prananda answered, "No, I prefer to practice my vina. You go and enjoy it." Later Indra returned and told Prananda, "The Buddha is half way through his life. Why don't you listen to the Dharma teachings with me?" Prananda replied, "I will continue practicing my vina. You go." Once more Indra returned and said, "The Buddha is ready to pass away. You had better come now," but Prananda preferred playing his lute.

To break Prananda's attachment and pride, the Buddha manifested as an Indian lute player carrying a lute made completely of lapis luzi. As he passed by the kingdom of the gandharvas, Prananda heard him playing by the palace gate, and feeling jealous said, "Let's compete to see who is the best." They sat down and both played perfectly. Then the Buddha said, "Let's cut one of the strings and then see who plays the best." They played equally well and began cutting more and more strings. When all the strings had been cut, the Buddha's emanation continued playing beautifully, while Prananda could not play. His pride was broken, and he asked, "Where did you learn to play like that?" The Buddha answered, "If you listen to the Dharma teachings of the Buddha, you will be able to play like this too." And so Prananda hurried off to received the dharma teachings.

The third kind of nirmanakaya, the born nirmanakaya, is unlike the supreme and created nirmanakaya since it has a body, and can take birth as a human or sometimes an animal. This kind of nirmanakaya does not just teach the Dharma but benefits beings through their activity or behavior.

Finally, there are various nirmanakaya emanations called *tulkus* in Tibetan, who are not supreme nirmanakayas. For example, the First Karmapa, *Tüsun Khyenpa* when he was at the end of his life, asked his students to look after his three centers at Tsurphu, Kamaga, Kampogangara. He told them that he would be reborn and come back and look after these places. Karma Pakshi was born later on, and said that he was the Karmapa. Since he had many miraculous powers, the power of clairvoyance, and so on, there was no doubt that he was the second Karmapa. His pupils were very happy, and his return helped them to continue to practice the Dharma. Consequently, when other lamas passed away, their students then went to high lamas and said, "We want our lama to return like Karmapa returned." In response high lamas used their clairvoyant powers to discover where the lama had been reborn, thus helping the student to practice the Dharma. Some tulkus can predict their own birth, as does the Karmapa, and others are recognized by other lamas.

Eventually, there were numerous tulkus in Tibet, some of whom had bad behavior, some who were unintelligent, which made some people wonder whether there was really anything special about tulkus. The tulku may have practiced very diligently and have lead a very pure life, and so be recognized lifetime after lifetime; however, sometimes a tulku practiced so well that he or she passed away and went to a pure realm. His or her pupils, not knowing this, would go to the Karmapa and ask about the reincarnation, and the Karmapa couldn't say, "He hasn't come back." Instead, the Karmapa would say something like, "Well, maybe this child could be him, and it will be beneficial if you choose him." Believing the child was the tulku, the students would find him, give him training, and his practice would benefit many beings.[40] So before the time of the First Karmapa the use of the word "nirmanakaya" for *tulku* was not used. But from this time on there have been many tulkus, and these make up the fourth kind of nirmanakaya.

THE DHARMADHATU WISDOM AS THE SVABHAVIKAKAYA

30. Thus mind, mentality, and sensory consciousnesses are transformed
Into the three kayas and their activity.
They are completely present within the mandala
of the complication-free dharmadhatu,
Without samsara, nirvana, or beginning,
Without being single or multiple.
This is called 'the essence kaya'(svabhavikakaya).

The origin of all the kayas, which we have been discussing, is the dharmakaya, more specifically, the aspect of the dharmakaya which is free from all mental fabrications, the svabhavikakaya. In the previous verses Rangjung Dorje has used three terms for mind rather interchangeably; *namshay* (consciousness) to refer to the eight consciousnesses and *yi* (mentality) and *sem* (mind). In this verse, however, he uses *sem* (mind) for the eighth consciousness, *yi* (mentality) for the seventh consciousness, and *namshay* for the six consciousnesses.

The eight consciousnesses are transformed into the three kayas: the ground consciousness becomes the dharmakaya, the afflicted consciousness becomes the sambhogakaya, and the other six consciousnesses become the nirmanakaya. Each kaya posses specific activities: the sambhogakaya assists pure beings to reach the ultimate achievement of Buddhahood, the nirmanakaya assists impure beings according to their capacities, and the dharmakaya has the wisdom and love that is the root of all three kayas. Thus, all their activities ultimately derive from the dharmakaya.

Although the dharmakaya is the source of the two wisdoms of the Buddha (the wisdom of the nature of phenomena (Tib. *ji ta ba*), and the wisdom of their variety (Tib. *ji nye pa*), and has love for all beings, and has the power of the Buddha's mind, yet it has no true reality. The dharmakaya is empty; its nature is the dharmadhatu, and it is free of mental fabrications. Although the sambhogakaya manifests a form with the thirty-two major and the eighty secondary signs of a supreme being, that manifestation has no true reality and is empty in nature. The nirmanakaya, although it acts to benefit beings, has a nature that is inseparable from the dharmadhatu.

All three of the kayas are beyond conceptual extremes. The dharmakaya is the dharmadhatu and is beyond any conceptual elaboration. Although the sambhogakaya only manifests to bodhisattvas, its essence is also beyond mental elaborations and therefore is also the dharmadhatu. Although the nirmanakaya manifests to impure beings in the form of the Shakyamuni Buddha, its essence is also beyond any mental elaborations and is therefore the dharmadhatu. For this reason all the kayas are nondifferentially one in the great mandala of the dharmadhatu which is called the "essence-kaya" or the "svabhavikakaya." The two aspects concerning realization of the true nature of phenomena are the svabhavikakaya and the dharmakaya with the svabhavikakaya being the aspect of emptiness and the dharmakaya being the aspect of clarity.

Shantideva (c. 675-725 C.E.) said that, because he taught that all phenomena are empty, some people replied, "If all phenomena are empty, then the Buddha is empty too, so that making offerings to the Buddha will not accumulate any merit. However, although the Buddha indeed has no reality, and is just like a dream, an illusory offering made to an illusory Buddha will still result in illusory merit, just as real merit would have arisen from real offerings to a real Buddha."

The three kayas have an empty essence and this emptiness is called the dharmadhatu. This dharmadhatu is the fifth wisdom of the five wisdoms and this wisdom is the absence of any inherent essence or reality. The Sanskrit word "dharmadhatu" was translated into

Tibetan as *chö ying* in which *ying* (Skt. *dhatu*) means "the expanse of space." Space is empty and has the quality of providing room so without space we could not move. Space allows us to walk, sit, or do any activity. It is combined with *chö* which is "dharma" so the dharmadhatu is "the space that enables things to happen."

Because the emotional afflictions (Skt. *kleshas*) are pervaded by the dharmadhatu, they don't have any solid reality and thus can be eliminated. If they were truly real, then one couldn't get rid of them. The positive qualities of love and wisdom can be developed, because they are pervaded by the dharmadhatu. If they were truly existing, then we wouldn't be able to change them. Thus, we are able to diminish the negative qualities and increase positive qualities because phenomena lack any true reality and are pervaded by dharmadhatu; in fact, these eight consciousnesses can be transformed into the five wisdoms because their nature is dharmadhatu.

Many names are given to the dharmadhatu: in the Hinayana it is called the "egolessness or selflessness of the individual," and in the Mahayana it is called "emptiness," but the actual characteristics are explained in the Madhyamaka Shentong school.[41] The Shentong tradition describes both the characteristics and the essence of the dharmadhatu. The word emptiness (Skt. *shunyata*) does not mean simply a dead vacuum; rather in the Shentong teachings the nature of emptiness is taught to be clarity or luminosity. Because of the power of this luminosity, dharmadhatu is given the name "the essence of the Tathagata" or tathagatagarbha which is often called Buddha-nature.

All sentient beings possess Buddha-nature, yet they are unable to realize the true nature of phenomena. This is because their dharmadhatu wisdom is covered by two obscurations: cognitive (not realizing the true nature of phenomena) and afflictive (the negative emotions). Just as the sky becomes clear when the clouds have vanished, the wisdom understanding of the true nature of phenomena appears when the afflictions have been removed. Due to the five wisdoms of mirror-like wisdom, the wisdom of equanimity, all-accomplishing wisdom, and discriminating wisdom, the realization concerning the truth of appearances is possible.

One cannot separate the eight consciousnesses and the dharmadhatu. The nature of the dharmadhatu is the eight consciousnesses and the nature of the eight consciousnesses is the dharmadhatu. This is the same for all two wisdoms; they are all imbued by the dharmadhatu. In Vajrayana meditation this is established by not meditating on the emptiness of external appearances, but meditating on the actual nature of the mind; one is taught to look directly at the mind.[42] For example, if we look at something, we obviously see its appearance in the mind; yet when we try to locate where this visual consciousnesses that is doing the looking is, we can't locate it. This is because the nature of the visual consciousness is empty; it is inseparable from dharmadhatu, and we call this "the inseparability of luminosity and emptiness." All the consciousnesses are completely pervaded by dharmadhatu, meaning their nature is also emptiness. The reason we can't find these consciousnesses is that their nature is insubstantial and constantly changing. In the Vajrayana tradition, this is the way we gain the direct recognition of the empty nature of the mind.

We can classify and divide these eight consciousnesses, as we have been doing, using deduction and reasoning; but we cannot actually isolate them when we look for them because they are the indivisibility of luminosity and emptiness. This emptiness is not a complete voidness, because luminosity is present, thus the process of mind seeing itself is this realization of emptiness. The mental consciousness can allow things to arise in the mind, but the mental consciousness is inseparable from the dharmadhatu and also empty by nature. When these consciousnesses are transformed into the wisdoms, the unity of wisdom and space[43] are established as inseparable.

The four wisdoms that have already been described are therefore pervaded by the dharmadhatu that is free of mental fabrications. The dharmakaya, sambhogakaya, and nirmanakaya are not new creations; they have always been there. It is this nature which is known as the fifth dharmadhatu wisdom that the eight consciousnesses are transformed into. This dharmadhatu wisdom is also a kaya: it is the svabhavikakaya or essence-kaya. The svabhavikakaya, like the dharmadhatu wisdom, is the absence of solid existence that provides space for the other three kayas to occur. That is the nature of the three kayas and why they are called the essence kayas. Thus Rangjung Dorje said, "multiple or single, this is called the essence kaya."

OTHER CLASSIFICATIONS OF THE WISDOMS AND THE KAYAS

31. In some other texts, the Victorious One
Teaches this to be the dharmakaya.
The mirror-wisdom is then described as the 'wisdom kaya'
And the other wisdoms as the two 'form kayas'

This section was written to clear away any doubts students might have. According to the capacities of beings the Buddha explained the kayas in various ways. Sometimes he spoke of only three kayas, not mentioning the svabhavikakaya, as it was included in the dharmakaya. Sometimes he spoke of the four wisdoms, not mentioning the dharmadhatu wisdom. Sometimes he taught that the dharmadhatu wisdom, the dharmakaya, and the mirror-like wisdom were part of a wisdom-kaya called the jnanakaya. Sometimes he taught that the wisdom of equality, discriminating wisdom, and all-accomplishing wisdom were part of the form-kaya called the rupakaya, which comprises the sambhogakaya and the nirmanakaya.

In other sutras and texts the essence-kaya was sometimes called the dharmakaya, because the dharmadhatu is the source of all the qualities of one's own realization and the ability to help other beings. Therefore the dharmadhatu wisdom was given the name the dharmakaya.

Finally, the mirror-like wisdom was sometimes called the wisdom kaya. Because it has the aspect of luminosity, the dharmadhatu is sometimes called the dharmakaya. The three wisdoms of equality, discriminating wisdom, and wisdom of all-accomplishment are almost always associated with the two form-kayas (the sambhogakaya and nirmanakaya).

Chapter 6

Summary of the Treatise

This chapter follows the tradition which originated at the great University of Nalanda. When the great *panditas* of Nalanda wrote commentaries, they described the different ways of relating to the Buddha's teachings. They proposed a method of presenting the subject in a brief summary, which was called "the leap of a tiger." Another method was giving every detail of a teaching word by word, which was called "the crawl of a turtle." There was also a third method of presenting a brief summary of the entire explanation, which was called "the lion returning." This text has been taught according to the crawling turtle method and this summary will use the lion returning method.

SUMMARY OF THE WISDOMS AND KAYAS

32. Buddhahood is the manifestation of the nature
Of the five wisdoms and four kayas.

When the eight consciousness are transformed into the five wisdoms and the four kayas, we become buddhas. Whichever terms are used, there are four kayas; the dharmakaya, sambhogakaya, nirmanakaya, and svabhavikakaya or jnanakaya.

THE TRANSFORMATION OF IMPURE TO PURE

33. That which possesses the stains of the mind,
mentality, and consciousness.
Is described as the ground consciousness.
That which is stainless, is the Buddha-nature.

Without the transformation of impure into pure, we are an ordinary being. As an ordinary being we have the mind and mentality and consciousness and they are stained with samsara. In this case, there is the ground consciousness is the basis of all samsara. The stains are a part of the consciousnesses which have already been described as impure, but the mind also has a pure aspect and this pure, stainless aspect is Buddha-nature.

34. The Buddha has taught that the truth of the path
Is the possession of the power of the Noble Ones,
That is born from the pure conceptualization,
That defeats impure thoughts.

We may ask how we actually transform the eight consciousnesses into the five wisdoms while on the path. The answer is to cultivate pure thoughts which will automatically defeat impure thoughts. By transforming the eight consciousnesses into the five wisdoms we come to understand the true nature of phenomena.

In a previous life, when there was a buddha who was also called Shakyamuni Buddha, the Buddha was a poor Brahmin. When he met the Shakyamuni Buddha, he felt great faith in him and wanted to make a connection, so he made an offering of rice soup, even though he didn't have a very nice bowl to put it in. He poured the soup into Shakyamuni's begging bowl, the Buddha drank it, and was very pleased. When that happened, the poor Brahmin made a wishing prayer to become just like that Shakyamuni Buddha; to have the exact same body, to teach the same doctrine, and to have the same name. In the future he did become the Shakyamuni Buddha. This demonstrates the necessity of having very pure thoughts and pure motivation.

This transformation happens through the five paths. First we develop trust and conviction in the Buddha's teachings and enter the path. At this first level of the path of accumulation of wisdom and merit, we begin to understand the Four Noble Truths are and how we can work without consciousnesses and so on. On the second path of junction we receive the teachings, contemplate them, and begin to meditate on them. By the third path of insight, our meditation becomes very pure and we actually see, for the first time, the true nature of phenomena and begin working on "the truth of the path," which are the ten bodhisattva stages. We follow the Noble Ones (Skt. *aryas*) who have realized emptiness. From this, the ultimate wisdom arises and this allows us to thoroughly understand the nature of phenomena.

THE REASON THIS TEXT WAS WRITTEN

35. The ignorant wander into the ocean of samsara
Because they have not realized this ultimate nature.
Other than with the boat of the Mahayana,
How could the other shore ever be reached?

Rangjung Dorje concludes by stating the reason that he wrote this text. Normally, we are in a state of delusion and ignorance and darkness. What we need to do is eliminate that state of ignorance and lack of understanding, by transforming the eight consciousnesses into the five wisdoms. If we don't understand the eight consciousnesses and the five wisdoms, then we won't know the path that has to be practiced, the goal that has to be attained, consequently, we will wander in samsara. The Tibetan word for samsara is *kor wa* which means "to go around," and indicates that in samsara things sometimes are good, sometimes they are bad, sometimes the disturbing emotions become weak, sometimes they become very strong—samsara is just a continuous cycle of happiness and suffering.

Samsara is described by the Buddha as being like an ocean, so we speak of the ocean of samsara. It is said to be like an ocean, because an ocean is very vast and very deep and very dangerous. In the time of the Buddha there weren't the boats that we have now, and the only way of traveling on the oceans was in sailboats. Voyages took a very long time, and at the time, it was easy for boats to sink and for passengers to drown. Beings wander on the ocean of samsara because they have not realized the ultimate nature of phenomena or the mind. Crossing it safely requires a great boat. This great vehicle is the Mahayana path. If we can enter and practice the Mahayana, we will be able to cross this ocean of samsara. There is no other means of doing so.

Rangjung Dorje describes his motivation by explaining that he wrote the *Treatise Distinguishing Consciousness from Wisdom* to explain the eight consciousnesses, and how they are obscured. But since these consciousnesses can ultimately be transformed into the five wisdoms, he describes them. Without understanding the eight consciousnesses and their transformation into the five wisdoms, the practitioner will remain in a state of darkness, and will not be able to attain freedom from samsara. Both happiness and suffering are experienced in samsara. Samsara is compared to a bee locked inside a pot. The bee sometimes flies to the top and is stopped by the lid and since there is nowhere to go, it flies to the bottom again repeating this pattern again and again. That really is what samsara is like. When sentient beings are in mental darkness, they wander around in samsara's ocean of misery. Rangjung Dorje writes that we need to be free of ignorance. We need to understand the teachings, to contemplate and to meditate on them. By doing this we will become free from ignorance, and will be able to cross the ocean of samsàra. He wrote this text so that others will understand the nature of all things, and be liberated from ignorance. He then concludes with a aspirational prayer:

THE CONCLUDING PRAYER

36. May this meaning be realized by everyone!

We need freedom from delusions of relative reality and the understanding of ultimate reality. If we meditate on the internal mind, we will directly experience its empty nature and its clarity. The realization of the true nature of mind is the direct path of the Vajrayana. Before we engage on this direct path, we must understand the difference between the various consciousnesses and wisdoms. This text does not discuss the Mahayana and Vajrayana meditation practices. It also does not discuss the Mahayana methods of proving the emptiness of all phenomena. The Mahayana sutras clarify the nature of the mind in terms of appearances arising in the mind and the empty nature of these appearances and this is taught in the text. The Vajrayana view of understanding the mind itself is also presented in the text. Therefore *Distinguishing Consciousness from Wisdom* is essential for understanding the Mahayana view as well as understanding Vajrayana practice. Rangjung Dorje then concludes with the prayer:

May everyone realize the meaning of this text.
May they understand by hearing the teachings
May they develop conviction through contemplation
and then be able to realize the meaning
of the Lord Buddha's teachings through meditation.

HOW THIS TREATISE WAS COMPOSED

The Treatise Distinguishing Consciousness and Wisdom was composed in the retreat center Dechen Teng, by Rangjung Dorje on the first day of the tenth lunar month of the year of the pig [the year 1323].

This treatise was composed by Rangjung Dorje, the Third Karmapa. Every Karmapa has his own special kind of activity to benefit his pupils. The First Karmapa excelled in meditation and established the monastic seats of the future Karmapas. The Second Karmapa had very powerful and frightening miraculous powers. The Fourth Karmapa Rolpay Dorje and the Fifth Karmapa Deshin Shegpa, had great worldly might and power. The Eighth Karmapa in contrast was uninvolved with worldly life and spent a simple life dedicated to meditation.

Rangjung Dorje, the Third Karmapa, was renowned as a great scholar of the sutras and the tantras. He had such great compassion, that when he passed away on the fourteenth day of the sixth lunar month in China, he appeared on the next day, the fifteenth, which is the full moon day, within the full moon. This was seen in Tibet as well as China. It gave rise to the tradition of painting Rangjung Dorje's image within a full moon disc. He wrote this text in Dechen Teng, which was a retreat center at Tsurphu, the principal seat of the Karmapa. The other two seats are Kampo Gangra, or Gangchi Rawa, which is in the east of Tibet, near the border with China, and Karma Gön which was in Kham. Gangchi Rawa had a great sangha, so it was like the body aspect, while Karma Gön had many scholars, so it was the speech aspect, while Tshurpu had many meditators, so it was the mind aspect.

Around five hundred meditators lived in Dechen Teng at Tshurpu, although since the Chinese Cultural Revolution in 1959 it is in ruins. Rangjung Dorje used to stay there and give teachings to the monks on retreat. It was during one of his residences there that he wrote this text. Therefore it was in a place dedicated to meditation, where there were many great meditators that he gave this teaching on consciousness and wisdom. Therefore this text will be of great benefit to those practicing meditation.

Notes

By Clark Johnson, Ph. D.

1. Mahamudra practice involves maintaining complete mindfulness and awareness in one's work, one's social activities, one's eating, sleeping, and so on. It also involves formal sitting meditation in which one looks directly at mind to see what is there.
2. In Tibetan Buddhism there is the practice of certain yogas in which one tries to clear out the subtle channels (Skt. *nadi* Tib. *tsa*) which are not anatomical, but more like meridians in acupuncture in which energies or winds (Skt. *prana*, Tib. *lung*) travel. These energies are closely related to thought so the practitioner does certain exercises and certain visualizations to enhance the mind in meditation. One example of these practices are the Six Yogas of Naropa.
3. When Tibetan scholars decided to divide the Buddhist teachings into several levels, they came up with the Hinayana, the Mahayana, and the Vajrayana. Unfortunately, the translation for Hinayana was "lower vehicle" and implied that it was somehow inferior. Thrangu Rinpoche makes the point that it is rather a 'fundamental vehicle' because no spiritual practice in the Mahayana or Vajrayana could be done without a thorough grounding and foundation practice of the Hinayana.
4. In a vast array of studies beginning with Hubel and Weisel, Western science has shown that the sense organs such as the eye do not simply send a picture of what is on the retina to the brain, but actually send processed information such as size, shape, and contour information to the brain where the picture is reconstructed. This information sent to the brain is not an accurate picture, however, with optical illusions being just one such example of the incorrectness of the picture sent. These sensory faculties, located in the brain, do work simultaneously and not in succession as suggested by the Buddhists.
5. *Salwa* is a quality of awareness of mind. This will be covered in greater detail in later chapters, but basically it can be shown that

the mind is "empty of inherent existence." This means that when we look for where thoughts originate, where they dwell, and where they go when a thought is completed, we cannot find them anywhere. They are not solid or real; otherwise they would have an origin, a place to dwell, and a place where they would go. However, we know that even though the mind is "empty" it has luminosity or clarity.

6. Egolessness of self (Tib. *dagme*) refers to the fact that when we look for mind i.e. where thoughts arise from, where they dwell, and where they vanish to, we can not find them. Furthermore, when we look for the consciousness and who is doing the thinking, we again find nothing is there and that the mind is rather an ever-changing stream of thoughts and feelings and not a solid self. We call this realization that we aren't a solid self or ego the wisdom of egolessness.
7. Aggregates (Skt. *skandha*, Tib. *pung po*) literally means "heaps" or "piles" as in a pile of rocks. In this context they are the five steps of perception. First, a visual image, sound, taste, or other sensory object contacts the sense faculty and this is the first aggregate of form. Second, there is a feeling of accepting or rejecting of this form which is the second aggregate of sensation. The perception is automatically classified as beautiful, pleasant, or desirable or as ugly, threatening, or undesirable, or as simply neutral. The sense perception, of course, is none of these—it is simply a sensory perception. Third, the sensory perception is identified so one identifies the perception as "a chair" or "my wife" or the like. This aggregate has been translated as identification or discrimination and this process, of course, involves past experience. After the sensory perception is identified, it is connected with previous conditioning and habitual patterns, in the fourth aggregate which is translated as formation. So one not only identifies the object, but all one's past history with the object and what it is relates to is part of this perception. The last aggregate is consciousness and this occurs when the perception enters the sixth mental consciousness as a mental object. Although we can divide these aggregates up as distinct units intellectually, they are actually a continuous, indivisible process of perception.

8. Negative emotions are kleshas which in Sanskrit means "pain, distress, and torment." This was translated as "afflictions" which is the closest English word to what causes distress. However, the Tibetan word for kleshas is *nyon mong* and these almost always refer to passion, anger, ignorance, jealousy, and pride which are actually negative or disturbing emotions so we prefer the translation negative or disturbing emotion since "afflictions" imply some kind of disability. *The Great Tibetan Dictionary* for example defines *nyon mong* as, "mental events that incite one to unvirtuous actions and cause one's being to be very unpeaceful."
9. The numbered verses are a translation of the original root text of Rangjung Dorje.
10. "To listen" to the teachings is the literal translation of the Tibetan *talwa.* Rinpoche has said that in this modern age this actually means "to study" the teachings.
11. Samsara may be divided into three realms. The lowest level is the desire realm (Skt. *kamadhatu,* Tib. *dö kham*) which is our ordinary existence in which we are dominated by desires. The next level is the form realm (Skt. *rupadhatu,* Tib. *zug kham*) which is being born without having a human body and being non-human because of having attained one of the four concentrations (Skt. *caturdhyana,* Tib. *samten shi*) in a previous life. Finally, there is the formless realm (Skt. *arupadhatu,* Tib. *zug kham)* where one is born completely as consciousness.
12. Interdependent origination (Skt. *pratityasamutpada,* Tib. *tendrel*) has been translated as interdependence and dependent origination. This is a very important concept since it explains how things happen without the existence of a god or creator. The Buddha suggested simply that everything in the world is related to everything else and when something happens it is due to the relationship between cause and effect. There are actually twelve steps (called chains) beginning with birth and going to the twelfth stage of death.
13. The word "nature" sometimes called "essence" is a translation of the Tibetan word *shi* (spelled *bzhi*). The "nature" of something is found in Aristotelian logic in the West. For example, water appears as solid and cold (ice), as transparent and fluid (water), and hot and vaporous (steam) and these can be said to be the

worldly appearances of water. Its essence or true nature is none of these appearances, but more like two hydrogen atoms combined with an oxygen atom. Another example is that people appear to us as having a whole variety of personalities and behaviors, but only an enlightened being is actually able to see their true nature which is buddha-nature.

14. Buddhists hold a view quite opposite to common sense or what is held in the West, which is that the world that we perceive is not really an accurate reflection of reality, but rather is just an illusion or an appearance. What we perceive is relative or conventional truth (Tib. *kunzop*), while an enlightened person can see the world "as it really is" or its ultimate truth (Tib. *dondam*). Ordinary beings see external phenomena as solid and real and experience existence as the continual ups and downs of samsara; while ultimately external phenomena is not this at all: it is empty.
15. Because one's likes and dislikes are based on past experience and habitual patterns which are stored in the ground consciousness, this needs to be present in perception when there is any recognition of the object. The afflicted consciousness is there because one's mind is still dualistic and this consciousness interprets everything in terms of "I" and "other."
16. The two different natures are the nature of external phenomena which is emptiness, but appears as solid real objects and the nature of the mind which is also emptiness, but it also has luminosity or an awareness. Because external phenomena have the same nature i.e. made of the same material, we can build roads, houses, airplane with external phenomena. However, mind has a different nature so we cannot build bridges and so on by simply thinking or dreaming them.
17. The complete title is "Explanation of the five sensory consciousnesses accomplishing the sensory objects, without any other creator."
18. The Madhyamaka school of Buddhism in the second century C.E. under the leadership of Nagarjuna developed an extremely complex and extensive set of logical arguments to show that all external phenomena is empty (Skt. *shunyata*). Thrangu Rinpoche tries to give a flavor of these arguments using a logical argument

known as "the single and multiple" showing that everything outside us that we see and think is solid and real is not inherently a "hand" or "chair" or "mountain" but rather our mind has superimposed this concept onto the object.

A modern example of this argument is that if we hit a brick wall with our fist, it will seem very solid and hurt a lot. Yet a physicist will tell us that the wall is actually 99.99% empty space and what little solid matter there is in the wall are atoms moving at incredible speeds and one can never even locate the position of these atoms. Furthermore, the wall is not red but simply lets our a radiation that the mind calls "red." In other words, on the relative level it is a solid, red brick wall because our mind has taken this impression and made it into a red brick wall. However, an advanced practitioner, such as Milarepa, used to move his body through solid objects because his mind had realized that, all such objects are, in fact, empty.

19. The word "look" is used here, but clearly this has nothing to do with sight. The word is used to contrast it with analyzing or examining which has an analytical, cognitive component which isn't present in "looking" at mind. So looking at mind implies direct and nonconceptual examination.

20. *Rangrig* is mind looking at itself. To understand this one has to understand the background of mahamudra practice. In mahamudra meditation one begins by first developing tranquillity meditation which trains the mind to focus on an object and stay with it without distraction or discursive conceptualization. One also develops vipashyana meditation which in the Vajrayana is discovering the true nature of phenomena. These two meditations are developed in formal sitting meditation while one also engages in trying to achieve complete mindfulness and awareness in post-meditation as well as accumulate as much merit as possible.

When these have been achieved to a high degree and one has done the four preliminary ngondro practices to develop devotion, purification, generosity, and devotion to one's guru, one then begins looking directly (nonconceptually) at mind itself to fully realize that mind and self are empty. This then is *rang rig* and one discovers that one cannot ever find the mind. Of course, what is doing the looking and what is being looked at, is the same: mind. Yet with extremely focused meditation it is possible to nonconceptually see the true nature of mind and its emptiness. This is mind seeing itself. For more details see Thrangu Rinpoche's *The Meditation of Mahamudra, Part I and Part II.*

21. The literal name of this heading is "The teaching is that the mind is birthless." Being birthless is a characteristic of phenomena which is empty of inherent existence.
22. In the Tibetan Kangyur it says, "Since the mind alone is the seed of all possibilities. It is this that unfolds samsara and nirvana."
23. This is a jewel that produces anything that is wished for. Thrangu Rinpoche says that in ancient times these did exist, but not any more. It is also a metaphor for attaining Buddhahood because all of one's wishes are fulfilled with the attainment Buddhahood.
24. Thrangu Rinpoche gives the example of Milarepa who meditated diligently and achieved the realization of emptiness. In the *Hundred Thousand Songs of Milarepa* there is the story of two academics who came to Milarepa's cave to discredit him. In reply he asked them if a rock in the cave was solid and they said, "Of course" whereupon Milarepa began moving his body through the rock. This was no trick, Milarepa had truly realized emptiness so this apparently solid world and appearances were no longer solid to him and he could freely move wherever he wanted.
25. A deva is the Sanskrit word for "god" and refers to someone who has reached a higher birth than a human birth, but since gods are still part of the six realms of samsara, they still have to receive dharma teachings to reach enlightenment.
26. Latencies (Skt. *vasana*, Tib. *pakchak*) These latent imprints that enter the eighth consciousness come through the seventh consciousness. These imprints are not apparently the experience itself, but are described more like dormant seeds which are away from soil, water, and sunlight. These imprints are either positive, negative, or neutral depending upon the whether they came from a positive, negative, or neutral thought or action. These imprints are then activated with experience and thus help create our

impression of the solidity of the world. There are actually several kinds of latencies: latencies which are associated with external sensory experiences, latencies which give rise to the dualistic belief of I and other, and positive and negative latencies due to our actions which cause us to continue to revolve around and around in samsara.

It should also be pointed out that different schools of Buddhism treated these latencies differently. The Mind-only school of the Cittamatrins founded by Asanga in the fourth century B.C.E. holds that there are eight consciousnesses (as does this treatise) and the latencies are responsible for us remaining in samsara and also experiencing the world as solid and not empty. The Madhyamaka followers of the Sautrantika school hold that there is an objective external reality and that are only seven consciousnesses and therefore no eighth consciousness. Basically they believe that the seventh consciousness receives these latencies and projects the outside world. Finally, the Madhyamaka followers of the Prasangika school do not hold that there is an external reality and that there is no seventh or eighth consciousness. They posit that the self is a conceptual stream that receives these latencies and is involved in the projection of external phenomena. The subject of different schools is, of course, extremely more complicated than this and there are present day sects in Tibet, which adhere to one or another of these views.

27. Western anatomical studies have shown that the sense organs process information and transmit this information to the brain. The retina of the eye, for example, has certain rods that transmit only when the object is round, other rods when it is square, others only when it is moving. So the picture the brain or mental consciousness receives is something like, "round, red, moving to the left, sharp edges, etc." and not just a picture of what falls on the retina (as happens on a film in a camera).
28. Pönlop Rinpoche has pointed out that anatomical texts describe very closely what Jamgon Kongtrul was describing. For example, the "fine copper hairs" are very similar to the microscopic hairs in the inner ear that are responsible for receiving sound.

29. Here we now have the joining of several strands of Buddhist philosophy: we have the emptiness of external phenomena on the ultimate level as explained by the Madhyamaka thinkers; we have these external objects as we experience them on the relative level, we have the luminosity of the mind as expounded by the Shentong school, we have the Cittamatra view that everything is mind and we have the Cittamatra view that the eighth consciousness has accumulated these latencies from beginningless time. So over beginningless time the eighth consciousness has received latencies that these empty external objects are solid and real and therefore when we perceive an object these latencies tell us that the external phenomena is solid and real, rather than empty. This has been expressed in the *Lankavatara* sutra with:

   The perception of external phenomena as reality
   Is caused by diverse thoughts
   Rooted in the psychic residue of past lives.
   This is the transitory mind.
   It creates all forms.
   What appears to be external reality
   Is actually nonexistent.

30. There are two basic ways to develop an understanding of emptiness: analytical meditation (Tib. je gom) and placement meditation (Tib. ne gom). In analytical meditation one reads (or listens to) a passage giving a logical argument supporting emptiness and then one goes into a seep shamatha meditation and contemplates this argument. In placement meditation one goes directly into deep shamatha meditation and then one "looks at mind" directly without any analysis and perceives its emptiness. The analytical method is associated with the sutra approach and placement meditation is associated with the mahamudra or dzogchen approach to meditation. For more details see Thrangu Rinpoche's *The Meditation of Mahamudra, Part I and Part II.*
31. Hungry ghosts (Skt. *preta*, Tib. *yidak*) are one of the six kinds of beings who inhabit samsara. These beings can only be seen by persons with special clairvoyance or who are highly spiritually

evolved. Thrangu Rinpoche teaches that because we ordinary can't see certain beings, such as hungry ghosts, does not necessarily mean they do not exist. In fact, the Buddha asked that paintings of the six realms be placed in temples and bodhisattvas would journey to these realms and came back and describe what they had seen. One can also see these realms as states of mind with each realm characterized a particular disturbing emotion. The gods are consumed with pride because they are the most revered beings, the jealous gods are not full gods so they are consumed with jealousy; humans are greatly concerned about material objects; animals are characterized by ignorance; the hungry ghosts are consumed by desire, and the hell beings are consumed by great hatred and aggression.

More specifically hungry ghosts in previous lifetimes were very stingy and miserly and motivated by great greed. They were reborn in the ghost realm without a body, but they can see food and water all around them, but have a very tiny throat said to be the size of the eye of a needle so they cannot fulfill their desire.

33. The difference between mind (Tib. *sem*) and mental factors (Tib. *sem yung*) is that mind is a collection of all that is present in thought, while mental factors are more like long-term dispositions. Mental factors may be positive such as the ten virtuous factors including faith, shame, and non-hatred; negative such as the six root afflictions including desire, anger, and pride and the twenty secondary afflictions such as jealousy, avarice, and dishonesty; and neutral such as the five aggregates, sleep, examination, and analysis. There are fifty-one mental factors in all according to most systems of Buddhist psychology. –Thrangu Rinpoche.
34. The ten virtuous deeds are abstaining from the three unvirtuous deeds of body: (1) killing, (2) stealing, and (3) sexual misconduct; the four unvirtuous deeds of speech: (4) lying, (5) slander, (6) harsh or unkind words, (7) useless or empty speech; and the three unvirtuous deeds of mind: (8) thoughts of greed, (9) malicious thoughts, and (10) holding the wrong view.
35. The Tibetan word for "meditation" is gom (spelled *sgom*) and the word for "habituation" is khom (spelled *goms*). So meditation has the root in the word for habituation.

36. Maudgalyayana was one of the Buddha's ten main disciples and he tried to lead the third council of the Buddhist teachings. His recitation of the Buddha's words was said to be blocked by demons so Maudgalyayana had to perform miracles to scare off these intruding demons.
37. The complete title of this section is "The mirror-wisdom explained as the dharmakaya, in terms of purifier and purified"
38. The complete title is "The mirror-wisdom: the result of purification—kaya and wisdom"
39. In the Mahayana literature there are only ten bodhisattva levels which are described in Figure 6. In the tantric (Vajrayana) literature there are thirteen levels which are the ten plus three more subtle stages of manifesting enlightenment.
40. Thrangu Rinpoche relates: "I have a personal experience of this. I am called Thrangu Tulku. When I first gave this some thought, I was perplexed. I thought, "Well, I know that I'm not Thrangu Tulku, but the Karmapa said that I was! The Karmapa knew my father's name and mother's name, even though I was born far away, and he didn't know my family." I thought about this a lot, and felt that it was all very strange. So one day I asked my *khenpo*, "I know I'm not the Thrangu Tulku, but I've been declared to be him. Why? Perhaps the real one will turn up some day." The khenpo said that there definitely wouldn't be anybody else, but that I knew what my own mind was like, and if I was certain I wasn't a tulku, then I wasn't one!

    This left me wondering, "What does all this mean?" until finally I understood. The Karmapa had given me the name of Thrangu Tulku, because it would be very beneficial for me. Otherwise, I would have either become a merchant like my father, or worked in the fields like my mother. Having been recognized as Thrangu Tulku, I became a monk, received teachings from many lamas and had the opportunity to practice the dharma. So he didn't declare me to be Thrangu Tulku because I was the actual tulku, but in order for me to carry on the work of the Thrangu Tulkus, which is what I am now doing.

    So we should understand that there is the supreme nirmanakaya, the created nirmanakayas and the born nirmanakayas, while in the tulku tradition of Tibet, there are superior tulkus, inferior tulkus, and finally counterfeit tulkus like myself!

41. Thrangu Rinpoche is one of the foremost scholars of the Shentong tradition, as was Jamgon Kongtrul and Rangjung Dorje before him.
42. This is mahamudra or dzogchen meditation. This is not as simple as it seems and requires years and years of training.
43. The fifth element is translated as "space" because it supports everything else. This is more like the concept of the fifth element (after earth, water, fire, air) of ether in Aristotelian logic rather than simply space.

A Brief Biography of Thrangu Rinpoche

Thrangu Rinpoche was born in Kham in 1933. At the age of five he was formally recognized by the Sixteenth Karmapa and the previous Situ Rinpoche as the incarnation of the great Thrangu tulku. Entering Thrangu monastery, from the ages of seven to sixteen he studied reading, writing, grammar, poetry, and astrology, memorized ritual texts, and completed two preliminary retreats. At sixteen under the direction of Khenpo Lodro Rabsel he began the study of the three vehicles of Buddhism while staying in retreat.

At twenty-three he received full ordination from the Karmapa. When he was twenty-seven Rinpoche left Tibet for India at the time of the Chinese military takeover. He was called to Rumtek, Sikkim, where the Karmapa had his seat in exile. At thirty-five he took the geshe examination before 1500 monks at Buxador monastic refugee camp in Bengal, and was awarded the degree of Geshe Lharampa. On his return to Rumtek he was named Abbot of Rumtek monastery and the Nalanda Institute for Higher Buddhist studies at Rumtek. He has been the personal teacher of the four principal Karma Kagyu tulkus: Shamar Rinpoche, Situ Rinpoche, Jamgon Kongtrul Rinpoche and Gyaltsab Rinpoche.

Thrangu Rinpoche has traveled extensively throughout Europe, the Far East and the USA; he is the abbot of Gampo Abbey, Nova Scotia, Canada, of Thrangu House, Oxford, in the UK. In 1984 he spent several months in Tibet where he ordained over 100 monks and nuns and visited several monasteries. He has also founded the monastery, Thrangu Tashi Choling in Bodhnath, a retreat center and college at Namo Buddha, east of the Katmandu Valley, and has established a school in Bodhnath for the general education of lay children and young monks. He built Tara Abbey in Katmandu. In October of 1999 he consecrate the College at Sarnath which will accept students from the different sects of Buddhism and will be available to western students as well.

Thrangu Rinpoche has given teachings in over 25 countries and is especially known for taking complex teachings and making them accessible to Western students. Thrangu Rinpoche is a recognized master of Mahamudra meditation.

More recently, because of his vast knowledge of the Dharma, he was appointed by His Holiness the Dalai Lama to be the personal tutor for the recently escaped 17th Karmapa.

The Glossary

Abhidharma (Tib. *chö ngön pa*) The Buddhist teachings are often divided into the Sutras (teachings of the Buddha), the Vinaya (teachings on conduct) and the Abhidharma (analyses of phenomena) which exist primarily as a commentarial tradition to the Buddhist teachings. There is not, in fact, an Abhidharma section within the Tibetan collection of the Buddhist teachings.

afflicted consciousness (Tib. *nyön yid*) The seventh consciousness. As used here it has two aspects: the immediate consciousness which monitors the other consciousnesses making them continuous and the klesha consciousness which is the continuous presence of self. See consciousnesses, eight.

afflictions These are another name for the kleshas or negative emotions. See kleshas

aggregrates, five (Skt. *skandha*) Literally, heaps. This is a five-fold category of phenomena—the five basic transformations that perceptions undergo when an object is perceived—form, feeling perception, formation, and consciousness. First is form which includes all sounds, smells, etc. everything that is not mind. The second and third are sensations (pleasant and unpleasant, etc.) and perception. Fourth is formation which actually include the second and third aggregates. The fifth is ordinary consciousness such as the sensory and mental consciousnesses.

alaya consciousness (Tib. *künshi namshe*) According to the Cittamatrin school this is the eighth consciousness and is often called the ground consciousness or store-house consciousness because it stores the latent karmic potentials.

analytical meditation (Tib. *je gom*) In the sutra tradition one begins by listening to the teachings which means studying the Dharma. Then there is contemplation of this Dharma which is analytical insight which is done by placing the mind in shamatha and putting the mind one-pointedly on these concepts.

arhat (Tib. *dra chom pa*) Accomplished Hinayana practitioners who have eliminated the negative emotions or kleshas. They are the fully realized shravakas and pratyekabuddhas.

arhatship The stage of having fully eliminated the klesha obscurations.

arya (Tib. *phag pa*) A person who has achieved direct realization of the true nature of reality. This person has achieved the third (path of insight) of the five paths.

Asanga (Tib. *thok me)* A fourth century Indian philosopher who founded the Cittamatra or Yogacara school and wrote the five works of Maitreya which are important Mahayana works. Also brother of Vasubhandu.

Atisha (982-1055 C.E.) A Buddhist scholar at Vikramashila University in India and came to Tibet at the invitation of the King of Tibet to overcome the damage done by Langdarma. He helped found the Kadam tradition.

atman Sanskrit for a permanent "self" which the Hindus believe exists after death.

Avalokiteshvara (Tib. *Chenrezig*) Deity of compassion who was known as the patron deity of Tibet and his mantra is OM MANI PADMa HUM.

ayatanas (Tib. *kye che*) These are the six sensory objects such as a sight, a sound, a smell, a taste, and body sensation; the six sense faculties of the visual sensory faculty, the auditory sensory faculty, etc. and the six sensory consciousnesses such as the visual consciousness, the auditory consciousness, etc. These make up the eighteen constituents of perception.

Bhrama A chief god in the form realm.

bodhisattva (Tib. *chang chup sem pa*) An individual who is committed to the Mahayana path of practicing compassion and the six paramitas in order to achieve Buddhahood and free all beings from samsara. More specifically, those with a motivation to achieve liberation from samsara for the sake of all sentient beings, the ten bodhisattva levels culminating in Buddhahood.

bodhisattva levels (Skt. *bhumi,* Tib. *sa*) The levels or stages a bodhisattva traverses to reach enlightenment. They usually are described as consisting of ten levels in the sutra tradition, and thirteen in the tantra tradition.

Bon (Tib.) The religion of Tibet before Buddhism was introduced which is still being practiced. A member is called a bonpo.

Brahmin A Hindu of the highest caste who usually performs the priestly functions for Hindu followers.

Buddha-nature (Skt. *tathagatagarba*, Tib. *de shin shek pay nying po*) The original nature present in all beings which when realized results in enlightenment. It is often called the essence of Buddhahood or enlightened essence.

Buddha Shakyamuni (Tib. *shakya thubpa*) The Shakyamuni Buddha, often called the Gautama Buddha, refers to the most recent historical Buddha, who lived between 563 and 483 B.C.E.

Candrakirti A seventh century Indian Buddhist scholar of the Madhyamaka school who is best known for founding the Prasangika subschool and writing two treatises on emptiness using logical reasoning.

Carvakas A philosophical school in India which reject the sacred scriptures and vedas, the belief in reincarnation and karma, and therefore advocated hedonism and doing whatever one wants in self-interest.

Chenresig (Skt. *Avalokiteshvara*) Deity of compassion. See Avalokiteshvara

Cittamatra school (Tib. *sem tam*) Usually translated as the Mind-only school. Founded by Asanga in the fourth century, one of the four major schools in the Mahayana tradition. The main tenet (to greatly simplify) is that all phenomena are mental events.

consciousnesses, sensory (Tib. *bang she*) These are the five sensory consciousnesses of sight, hearing, smell, taste, touch, and body sensation.

consciousnesses, eight (Skt. *vijnana*, Tib. *nam she tsog gye*) The five sensory consciousnesses of sight, hearing, smell, taste, touch, and body sensation; plus the sixth mental consciousness, the seventh afflicted consciousness, and the eighth ground consciousness.

conventional wisdom (Tib. *kun sop*) There are two truths: relative and absolute. Relative truth is the perception of an ordinary (unenlightened) person who sees the world with all his or her projections based on the false belief in ego.

clarity (Tib. *salwa*) Also translated as luminosity. The nature of mind is that it is empty of inherent existence, but the mind is not just voidness, completely empty because it has this clarity which is aware or the knowing of mind. So clarity is a characteristic of the emptiness (*shunyata*) of mind and distinguishes this from a simple voidness.

definitive meaning (Tib. *ngedon*) The Buddha's teachings that state the direct meaning of dharma. They are not changed or simplified for the capacity of the listener. In contrast to the provisional meaning.

dependent origination (Skt. *pratityasamutpada*, Tib. *ten drel*) The principal that nothing exists independently, but comes into existence only in dependence on various previous causes and conditions. There are twelve successive phases of this process that begin with ignorance and end with old age and death.

desire realm (Tib. *dö kham*) The abode of the six realms of samsara, so called because its inhabitants are continually tempted by desire.

deva (Tib. *lha*) Sanskrit for god. In this book it refers to a more highly evolved being who is still part of samsara and therefore in need of Dharma teachings to reach enlightenment.

dharma (Tib. *chö*) Dharma has two main meanings: any truth such as the sky is blue, and the teachings of the Buddha as used in this text.

dharani A short sutra containing mystical formulas of knowledge that are symbolic. They are usually longer than mantras.

dharmadhatu (Tib. *chö ying*) The all-encompassing, unoriginated, beginningless space out of which all phenomena arise. The Sanskrit means "the essence of phenomena" and the Tibetan means "the expanse of phenomena" but usually it refers to the emptiness which is the ground out of which phenomena arises.

dharmakaya (Tib. *chö ku*) One of the three bodies of Buddhahood. It is enlightenment itself, that is, wisdom beyond reference point. See kayas, three.

dharmata (Tib. *chö nyi*) Often translated as "suchness" or "the true nature of phenomena" or "things as they are." It is phenomena they really are and as seen by a completely enlightened being, without any distortion or obscuration. One can say it is true "reality."

disturbing emotion (Tib. *nyon mong*) Literally, poison. Translated as "afflictions" or "defilements" by some, but in this text as "negative emotions." The three main poisons are passion or desire, aggression or anger, and ignorance. The five kleshas are the three above plus pride and jealousy.

doha (Tib. *gur*) A spiritual song that is spontaneously composed by a Vajrayana practitioner. It usually has nine syllables per line.

T̲üsum Khyenpa (1110-1193 C.E.) The First Karmapa who was a student of Gampopa and founded the Karma Kagyu lineage. He is also known for founding the tulku system in Tibet.

dzogchen (Skt. *mahasandhi*) Also known as the "great perfection" or atiyoga. It is the highest of the nine yanas according to the Nyingma tradition. This meditation involves looking directly at mind.

eighteen constituents of perception See ayatanas.

emptiness (Skt. *shunyata,* Tib. *tong pa nyi*) Also translated as voidness. The Buddha taught in the second turning of the wheel of dharma that external phenomena and internal phenomena or concept of self or "I" have no real inherent existence and therefore are "empty."

egolessness (Tib. *dag me*) Also called selflessness. There are two kinds of egolessness—the egolessness of other, that is, the emptiness of external phenomena and the egolessness of self, that is, the emptiness of a personal self.

five aggregates (Skt. *skandha*) Literally heaps. The aggregates are the five basic constituents of perception that perceptions undergo when an object is perceived. These are form, feeling, identification, formation, and consciousness.

five sensory consciousnesses These are the sensory consciousnesses of sight, hearing, smell, taste, touch, or body sensation.

five paths (Tib. *lam nga*) Traditionally, a practitioner goes through five stages or paths to enlightenment. These are (1) The path of accumulation which emphasizes purifying one's obscurations and accumulating merit. (2) The path of junction or application in which the meditator develops profound understanding of the Four Noble Truths and cuts the root to the desire realm. (3) The path of insight or seeing in which the meditator develops greater insight and enters the first bodhisattva level. (4) The path of meditation in which the meditator cultivates insight in the second through tenth bodhisattva levels. (5) The path of fulfillment or no more learning which is the complete attainment of Buddhahood.

five dhyana buddhas (Tib. *gyel wa rig nga*) The sambhogakaya deities of Vairocana, Akshobhya, Ratnasambhava, Amitabha, and Amoghasiddhi. Each one represents one of the five wisdoms.

five wisdoms (Tib. *yeshe nga*) Upon reaching enlightenment, the eight consciousnesses are transformed into the five wisdoms: the mirror-like wisdom, discriminating wisdom, the wisdom of equality, the all-accomplishing wisdom, and the dharmadhatu wisdom.

form kayas (Skt. *rupakaya*, Tib. *zuk ku*) The sambhogakaya and the nirmanakaya. See the kayas, three.

form realm (Tib. *zuk kham*) The second of the three realms. In the form realm there are seventeen heavenly realms in which beings have bodies of light. See the realms, three.

formless realm (Tib. *zuk me kham*) The highest of the three realms and the abode of an unenlightened being who has practiced the four absorptions of infinite space, infinite consciousness, nothing-at-all, and neither cognition nor non-cognition. See the realms, three.

Four Noble Truths (Tib. *pak pay den pa shi*) The Buddha began teaching at Saranath, India on the four truths. These are the truth of suffering, the truth of the cause of suffering, the truth of the cessation of suffering, and the eight-fold path which make up the foundation of Buddhism.

gandharva (Tib. *dri za*) A class of deities who are celestial musicians and who live on odors.

Gelug school One of the four main schools of Tibetan Buddhism founded by Tsong Khapa (1357-1419 C.E.). His Holiness the Dalai Lama heads this lineage.

geshe (Tib.) A scholar who has attained a doctorate in Buddhist studies. This usually takes twelve to eighteen years to attain.

ground consciousness (Tib. *kunshi namshe*) The eighth consciousness which has the function of storing all the latent karmic imprints of experience. See consciousness, eight.

Hinayana (Tib. *tek pa chung wa*) Literally, the lesser vehicle. The term refers to the first teachings of the Buddha which emphasized the careful examination of mind and its confusion. Also called the Theravadin path and is the foundation of all Buddhist practice.

hungry ghosts (Skt. *preta*, Tib. *yadik*) One of the six types of beings of samsara. Hungry ghosts do not have material bodies, but see all the food and water around them, but cannot eat or drink it. As a result they are always starving and thirsty and this is the result of excessive greed in their previous lifetimes. See the six realms of samsara.

Indra (Tib. *brgua byin*) The chief god of the desire realm said to reside on the top of Mt. Meru.

insight meditation (Skt. *vipashyana*, Tib. *lhak tong*) Meditation that develops insight into the nature of phenomena. In the Theravada tradition this involves observing every thought in daily life. In the Vajrayana it involves more a close examination of the emptiness of phenomena. The other main meditation 's shamatha meditation.

interdependence (Skt. *pratityasamutpada*, Tib. *tren drel*) Also called dependent origination. The principal that nothing exists independently, but comes into existence only on dependency of various previous causes and conditions. There are twelve successive phases of this process that begin with ignorance and end with old age and death.

jealous gods (Skt. *asura*, Tib. *lha ma yin*) A type of being residing in the six realms of samsara who are characterized as being very jealous.

jnana (Tib. *yeshe*) Enlightened wisdom which is beyond dualistic thought.

Kadam (Tib.) One of the major schools in Tibet. It was founded by Atisha (993-1054 C.E.). A follower is a Kadampa.

Kagyu (Tib.) One of the four major schools of Tibetan Buddhism founded by Marpa and headed by His Holiness, the Karmapa.

The other three schools are the Nyingma, the Sakya, and the Gelug schools.

Kamalashila An eighth century scholar in India who was a student of Shantarakshita and is best known for coming to Tibet and debating and defeating the Chinese scholar Hashang Mahayana at Samye monastery and then writing the *Stages of Meditation*.

Karma Kagyu (Tib.) One of the eight schools of the Kagyu lineage of Tibetan Buddhism which is headed by His Holiness Karmapa.

Kangyur (Tib.) The 104 volume Tibetan collection of the Buddha's words. The other great collection is the Tengyur which contains the commentaries on the Buddha's teachings.

karma (Tib. *lay*) Literally, "action." An universal law of cause and effect in which wholesome actions eventually result in improved circumstances, and negative actions eventually result in negative circumstances.

Karma Pakshi (1206-1283 C.E.) The Second Karmapa who was known for his miraculous activities.

Karmapa The title of seventeen successive incarnations of Dusum Khyenpa who has headed the Karma Kagyu school of Tibetan Buddhism.

kayas, three (Tib. *ku sum*) A buddha has three bodies: the nirmanakaya, sambhogakaya, and dharmakaya. The dharmakaya or "truth body," is the complete enlightenment or complete wisdom of a buddha, which is unoriginated wisdom beyond form that manifests as the sambhogakaya and the nirmanakaya. The sambhogakaya or the "enjoyment body," manifests only to bodhisattvas in the pure realms and the nirmanakaya, or "emanation body," manifests in the world, and in this context, as the Shakyamuni Buddha.

klesha See disturbing emotions.

klesha consciousness (Tib. *nyön yid*) The seventh consciousnesses which is responsible for the constant presence of ego or "I." See consciousnesses, eight.

wisdom of the nature of phenomena (Tib. *ji ta ba*) This is transcendent knowledge (jnana) of the true nature of reality, not as it appears in samsara.

wisdom of the variety of phenomena (Tib. *ji nye pa*) This is the transcendent knowledge (jnana) of the variety of phenomena.

lama (Skt. *guru*) A spiritual teacher.

latent karmic imprints (Skt. *vasana*, Tib. *pakchak*) Every action that a person does, has an imprint which is stored in the eighth consciousness. These latencies express themselves later by leaving the eighth consciousness and entering the sixth consciousness upon being activated by causes and conditions.

luminosity (Tib. *salwa*) In the Vajrayana everything is empty, but this emptiness is not completely void because it has luminosity. Luminosity, also called clarity allows all phenomena to appear and is a characteristic of emptiness (Skt. *shunyata*).

Madhyamaka (Tib. *du ma*) A philosophical school founded by Nagarjuna in the first century C.E. Its main tenant is that everything is empty of self-nature.

mahamudra (Tib. *cha ja chen po*) Literally, "great seal" meaning that all phenomena are sealed by the primordially perfect true nature. This form of meditation is traced back to Saraha (10th century C.E.) and was passed down in the Kagyu lineage through Marpa. It is, to greatly simplify, the meditation of examining mind directly.

mahasiddha (Tib. *drup thop chen po)* A practitioner who has a great deal of realization. These were particularly Vajrayana practitioners who lived in India between the eight and twelfth century and practiced tantra. The biography of some of the most famous mahasiddha is found in *The Eighty-four Mahasiddhas*.

Mahayana (Tib. *tek pa chen po*) Literally, the great vehicle. These are the teachings of the second turning of the wheel of dharma, which emphasize shunyata, compassion, and Buddha-essence.

Maitreya (Tib. *jampa*) In this text it refers to the bodhisattva Maitreya who lived at the time of the Buddha. Maitreya is presently residing in the Tushita pure realm until he becomes the fifth buddha of this eon.

mandala (Tib. *chin kor*) A diagram used in various Vajrayana practices, which usually has a central deity and four directions. It also denotes a sacred location such as the mandala of the dharmakaya and this is how it is used in this text.

Manjushri (Tib. *yang*) A meditational deity representing discriminative awareness (prajna) known for knowledge and learning. Usually depicted as holding a sword in the right hand and scripture in the left.

mental consciousness (Tib. *yid kyi namshe*) The sixth consciousness responsible for analyzing the sensory perceptions of the five sensory consciousnesses. See consciousnesses, eight.

Maudgalyayana One of the Buddha's ten main disciples.

mental factors (Tib. *sem yung*) Mental factors are contrasted to mind in that they are more long-term propensities of mind. These include eleven virtuous factors such as faith, detachment, and equanimity, and the six root defilements such as desire, anger, and pride, and the twenty secondary defilements such as resentment, dishonesty, harmfulness.

mind poisons (Tib. *duk*). Literally means "poison" but is usually translated as "defilements" in this text. The three main poisons are passion or desire, aggression or anger, and ignorance. The five poisons are the three above plus pride and envy or jealousy.

Middle-way (Tib. *u ma*) or Madhyamaka School. A philosophical school founded by Nagarjuna in the first century C.E. and based on the Prajnaparamita sutras of emptiness.

Milarepa (1040-1123 C.E.) Milarepa was a student of Marpa who attained enlightenment in one lifetime. His student Gampopa founded the (Dagpo) Kagyu lineage.

Mind-only school. Also called the Cittamatra school. This is one of the major schools in the Mahayana tradition founded in the fourth century by Asanga that emphasized everything is mental display.

nadi (Tib. *tsa*) Subtle channels through which the subtle energies (vayu) flow.

Nagarjuna (Tib. *ludrup)* An Indian scholar in the first century who founded the Madhyamaka philosophical school which emphasized emptiness.

Nalanda A great monastic Buddhist university from the fifth to the tenth century located near modern Rajagriha which was the seat of the Mahayana teachings. Many great Buddhist scholars taught there.

Naropa (956-1040 C.E.) An Indian pandita who is best known for transmitting many Vajrayana teachings to Marpa who later took these teachings back to Tibet to help found the Kagyu lineage.

nirmanakaya (Tib. *tulku*) There are three bodies of the Buddha and the nirmanakaya or "emanation body" manifests in this world and in this context manifested as the Shakyamuni Buddha. See kayas, three.

nirvana (Tib. *nyangde*) Literally, extinguished. Beings who live in samsara can, with spiritual practice, attain a state of enlightenment in which all false ideas and conflicting emotions have been extinguished. This is called nirvana.

Noble Truths, Four See Four Noble Truths.

Nyingma (Tib.) The oldest school of Buddhism in Tibet based on the teachings of Padmasambhava and others in the eighth and ninth centuries of this era.

obscurations, two (Tib. *drippa nyi*) The obscuration of conflicting emotions and the obscuration of knowledge.

Padmasambhava (Tib. *Guru Rinpoche*) He was invited to Tibet in the eighth century C.E. and is known for pacifying the nonBuddhist forces and founding the Nyingma lineage.

pandita (Tib. *pandita*) A great scholar.

paramita, six (Tib. *parol tu chinpa*) Sanskrit for "perfections" and the Tibetan literally means "gone to the other side." These are the six practices of the Mahayana path: Transcendent generosity, transcendent discipline, transcendent patience, transcendent exertion, transcendent meditation (*dhyana*), and transcendent knowledge (*prajna*). The ten paramitas are these plus skilful means, aspirational prayer, power, and pure wisdom (Tib. *yeshe*).

path The path refers to the process of attaining enlightenment. Path may also refer to part of the threefold logic of ground, path, and fruition.

paths, five See five paths.

placement meditation This is the meditation of directly observing the mind without engaging in any analytical or intellectual activity. This meditation is associated with mahamudra meditation and it contrasts to analytical meditation.

poisons, three (Tib. *duk sum*) The three poisons or major defilements also called desire or attachment, anger or aggression, and ignorance or bewilderment.

prajna (Tib. *sherab*) In Sanskrit prajna means "perfect knowledge" but here the word means more "intelligence" because it can refer to simply mastering a subject intellectually as well as full realization of the ultimate nature of reality. In this treatise it usually means the wisdom of seeing things from a non-dualistic view.

Prajnaparamita (Tib. *sherab chi parol tu chin pa*) The Buddhist literature outlining the Mahayana path and emptiness written mostly around the second century.

Pramana (Tib. *tse ma*) Sometimes called "valid cognition." It is the study of the theory of knowledge.

pratyekabuddha (Tib. *rang sang gye*) Literally, solitary realizer. A realized Hinayana practitioner who has achieved the wisdom of the nature and the wisdom of the variety of phenomena, but is not committed to the bodhisattva path of helping all other beings.

prana (Tib. *bindu*) Life supporting energy.

provisional meaning (Tib. *drang dön*) The teachings of the Buddha which have been simplified or modified to the capabilities of the audience. This contrasts with the definitive meaning.

pure realm (Tib. *dag zhing*) Realms created by buddhas which are totally free from suffering and dharma there can be received directly. These realms are presided over by various buddhas such as Amitabha, Avalokiteshvara, and Maitreya who presides over Tushita.

Rangjung Dorje (1284-1339 C.E.) The Third Karmapa known for his great scholarship. He wrote the *Aspirational Prayer for Mahamudra*, the *Profound Inner Meaning*, a *Treatise on Buddha-essence*, and this text.

realms, three (Tib. *ku sum*) The lowest realm is the desire realm where beings are dominated by desire. It comprises humans, animals, and hungry ghosts. The next realm is the form realm where beings don't have a body and are free of gross pain and pleasure. The highest realm is the formless realm, which can only be reached as the result of a high previous meditational accomplishment.

relative truth (Tib. *kün sop*) There are two truths: relative or conventional truth, and absolute or ultimate truth. Relative truth is the perception of an ordinary (unenlightened) person who sees the world through false ego-based projections.

rinpoche (Tib.) Literally, very precious. A term of respect for a Tibetan lama who is a recognized incarnation.

rishi A holy Hindu sage or saint.

rupakaya (Tib. *zuk kyi ku*) The form bodies which encompass the sambhogakaya and the nirmanakaya.

Sakya One of the four major schools of Tibetan Buddhism. It was established by Drogmi Lotsawa in the eleventh century.

Shakyamuni Buddha (Tib. *shakya tubpa*) The Shakyamuni Buddha, often called the Gautama Buddha, refers to the latest Buddha who lived between 563 and 483 B.C.E.

samadhi (Tib. *tin ne zin*) Also called meditative absorption or one-pointed meditation. The highest form of meditation.

shamatha (Tib. *shinay*) A basic meditation practice that tames the mind and allows it to stay or rest on a point without being distracted. It is also called tranquillity or basic sitting meditation. The other basic meditation is vipashyana or insight meditation.

sambhogakaya (Tib. *long ku*) See the three kayas.

samsara (Tib. *khorwa*) Conditioned existence which is characterized by suffering because one is still afflicted by passion, aggression, and ignorance. It is contrasted to nirvana.

sangha (Tib. *gendun*) These are the companions on the path. They may be the persons on the path or the noble sangha, which are the realized bodhisattvas.

Shantarakshita (eighth century C.E.) An abbot of Nalanda University who was invited by King Trisong Detsen to come to Tibet. He established Samye Monastery and thus helped introduce Buddhism in Tibet.

Shantideva (675-725 C.E.) A great bodhisattva who lived in the seventh and eighth century in India known for his two works on the conduct of a bodhisattva.

Saraha One of the eighty-four mahasiddhas of India who was known for his spiritual songs about mahamudra.

Shariputra (Tib. *shari pu*) One of the Buddha's ten main disciples. He is known for his intelligence and when the sutras say, "Thus have I heard..." it is Shariputra who recited this sutra.

shastra (Tib. *tenchö*) The Buddhist teachings are divided into words of the Buddha (the sutras) and the commentaries by others on his works (shastras).

Sautrantika school (Tib. *do de pa*) One of the four major schools of Indian Buddhism. This is a Hinayana school.

self-knowledge (Tib. *rang rig*) This is a high meditation in which one looks directly at mind itself with no conceptualization to determine the characteritics of reality.

selflessness (Tib. *dag me*) Also called egolessness. In two of the Hinayana schools (Vaibhashika and Sautrantika) this referred exclusively to the fact that "a person" is not a real permanent self, but rather just a collection of thoughts and feelings. In two of the Mahayana schools (Cittamatra and Madhyamaka) this was extended to mean there was no inherent existence of external phenomena as well.

salwa Tibetan for luminosity. In the Vajrayana everything is void, but this voidness is not completely empty because it has luminosity. Luminosity or clarity allows all phenomena to appear and is a characteristic of emptiness (shunyata).

Shentong school (Tib.) The Madhyamaka or Middle-way school divided into two major schools: the Rongtong which maintains emptiness is devoid of inherent existence and Shentong which maintains emptiness is indivisible from luminosity.

six realms of samsara (Tib. *rikdruk*) These are the possible types of rebirths for beings in samsara and are: the god realm in which gods have great pride, the asura realm in which the jealous gods try to maintain what they have, the human realm which has the possibility of achieving enlightenment, the animal realm characterized by stupidity, the hungry ghost realm characterized by great craving, and the hell realm characterized by aggression.

skandha (Tib. *pung po*) Literally, heaps. The five basic transformations that perceptions undergo when an object is perceived. These are form, feeling, perception, formation, and consciousness. First is form which includes all sounds, smells, etc. The second and third are sensations (pleasant and unpleasant, etc.) and identification. Fourth is mental events which actually include the second and third aggregates. The fifth is ordinary consciousness such as the sensory and mental consciousnesses.

spiritual song (Skt. *doha*) A religious song spontaneously composed by a Vajrayana practitioner. It usually has nine syllables per line.

shravaka (Tib. *nyan tho*) Literally, those who hear. A type of realized Hinayana practitioner (*arhat*) who has achieved the realization of the nonexistence of personal self.

subtle channel (Skt. *nadi*, Tib. *tsa*) Subtle non-anatomical channels that psychic energies or winds (Skt. *prana*, Tib. *lung*) travel through.

shunyata (Tib. *tong pa nyi*) Usually translated as voidness or emptiness. The Buddha taught in the second turning of the wheel of Dharma that all external phenomena and all internal phenomena such as the concept of self or "I" have no real inherent existence and, therefore, are "empty."

sutra (Tib. *do*) Hinayana and Mahayana texts that are the Buddha's words. They are often contrasted with the tantras, which are the Buddha's Vajrayana teachings, and the shastras, which are commentaries by otherson the words of the Buddha.

sutrayana The sutra approach to achieving enlightenment which includes the Hinayana and the Mahayana.

svabhavikakaya (Tib. *ngo bo yi kyi ku*) The essence body, which refers to the dharmakaya.

tantra (Tib. *gyü)* One can divide Tibetan Buddhism into the sutra tradition and the tantra tradition. The sutra tradition primarily involves the academic study of the Mahayana sutras and the tantric path primarily involves practicing the Vajrayana practices. The tantras are primarily the texts of the Vajrayana practices.

tathagata (Tib. *deshin shekpai*) Literally, "those who have gone to thusness." A title for the Buddha.

tathagatagarba (Tib. *deshin shekpai nying po*) Also called Buddha-essence or Buddha-nature. The seed or essence of tathata (suchness).

Tengyur (Tib.) The great Tibetan collection of 108 works of the commentaries (shastra) of the Buddhist works. See Kangyur.

terma (Tib.) Literally, hidden treasure. Works which were hidden by great bodhisattvas and later rediscovered. They might be actual physical texts or they may come from "the sky" as transmissions from the sambhogakaya. A discoverer of these texts is called a terton.

Theravada (Tib. *neten depa*) Specifically a follower of the Thereavad school of the Hinayana. Here refers to the first teachings of the Buddha which emphasized the careful examination of mind and its confusion.

three realms See realms, three.

Tilopa (928-1009 C.E.) One of the eighty-four mahasiddhas who became the guru of Naropa. These teachings became the basis of the Kagyu lineage in Tibet.

tranquillity meditation (Skt. *shamatha*, Tib. *shinay*) A basic meditation practice that tames the mind and allows it to stay or rest on a point without being distracted. It is also called tranquillity or basic sitting meditation. The other basic meditation is vipashyana or insight meditation.

Tripitaka (Tib. *de nö sum*) Literally, the three baskets. There are the sutras (the narrative teachings of the Buddha), the Vinaya (a code for monks and nuns) and the Abhidharma (philosophical background of the dharma).

tulku (Tib., Skt. *nirmanakaya*) A manifestation of a buddha that is perceived by an ordinary person. The term has commonly been used for a discovered rebirth of any teacher.

Tushita (Tib. *gan dan*) This is one of the heaven abodes of the Buddha. Tushita is in the sambhogakaya and, therefore, does not have a specific location.

twelve deeds of the Buddha The life of the Buddha is often summarized in twelve major deeds.

two truths (Skt. *dvisatya*, Tib. *den pa gnyi*) There is the conventional or relative truth which is the world as we normally experience it with solid objects. The other truth is ultimate or absolute truth which is mind free of all obscurations, defilements, and inherently empty.

ultimate level (Tib. *dondam*) This ultimate truth which can only be perceived by an enlightened individual is that all phenomena both internal (thoughts and feelings) and external (the outside physical world) does not have any inherent existence.

Upanishads Pre-Buddhist Hindu religious texts dating from the seventh century B.C.E.

Vaibhashika (Tib. *bye brag smra ba*) One of four main Hinayana schools, with the other three being the Sautrantika, Cittamatra, and Madhyamaka schools. This school held that matter was real or independently existing and was composed of particles and that time was real and composed of moments which then composed consciousness.

vajra (Tib. *dorje*) Usually translated "diamond like." A hand held implement used during certain Vajrayana practiced and ceremonies or a quality that is so pure and so enduring that it is like a diamond.

vajra posture (Tib. *dorje duk stang*) The full lotus meditation posture that follows the seven points of Vairocana.

Vajrayana (Tib. *dorje tek pa*) There are three major traditions of Buddhism (Hinayana, Mahayana, Vajrayana) which are based on the tantras. The Vajrayana emphasizes the clarity aspect of phenomena, and is mainly practiced in Tibet.

Vasubandhu (Tib. *yik nyen*) A great fourth century Indian scholar who was Asanga's brother and wrote the Hinayana work the *Abidharmakosha* explaining the Abhidharma.

Vinaya (Tib. *dul wa*) The Buddha's teaching concerning proper conduct. There are seven main precepts that may be observed by lay persons, 125 that are observed by monks, and 320 that are observed by nuns.

vipashyana meditation (Tib. *lhag tong*) Sanskrit for "insight meditation" in which one develops insight into the nature of mind. The other main meditation is tranquillity or shamatha meditation.

wish-fulfilling jewel (Tib. *yid shin norbu*) A jewel said to exist in the naga or deva realms which gave the owner whatever he or she wanted. Now used mostly metaphorically.

yana (Tib. *tek pa*) Literally, vehicle. Refers here to a level of teaching. There are three main yanas. See Hinayana, Mahayana, and Vajrayana.

yoga Literally, union. In this text it refers to special movement and breathing exercises that are done to enhance meditation by clearing the subtle channels.

The Glossary of Tibetan Words

Note: There is no standard way to pronounce Tibetan.

Pronounced	Spelled	English
bang she	dbang shes	sensory conscious.
bardo thodrol	bard do'ithos grol	"Book of the Dead"
bon	bon	Bon religion
brgua byin	brgua byin	Indra
bye brag smtra	bye brag smra ba	Vaibashika
cha ja chen po	phyag rgya chen po	mahamudra
chang chup sem pa	byan chub sems dpa'	bodhisattva
che rim	bskyed rim	generation stage
Chenresig	span ras gzig	Avalokiteéhvara
chin kor	dkyil 'khor	mandala
chö	chos	dharma
chö chi ku	chos kyi sku	dharmakaya
chö ngön pa	chos mngon pa	Abhidharma
chö nyi	chos nyid	dharmata
chö ying	chos dbyings	dharmadhatu
dag me	dbag med	selflessness
dag zhing	dag zhing	pure realm
den pa gnyi	bden pa gnyis	two truths
de nö sum	sde snod gsum	Tripitaka
deshin shekpai	de bzhin gshegs pa	tathagatas
deshin shek pay nying po	de bzin gsheg pai' nying po	buddha-nature
do	mdo	sutra
do de pa	mdo sde pa	Sautrantika
dö kham	'dod khams	desire realm
dondam	don dam	ultimate nature
dorje	rdo rje	vajra
dorje tek pa	rdo rje theg pa	Vajrayana
dra chom pa	dgra bcom pa	arhat
dri za	dri za	gandarva
drubgya	sgrub rgyud	practice lineage
drup thop chenpo	grub thob chen po	mahasiddha
duk	dug	poisons
duk sum	dug gsum	three poisons
du ma	dbu ma	Madhyamaka
dul ma	'dul ba	Vinaya
dzog chen	rdzogs chen	great perfection
gan dan	dga' ldan	Tushita
Gelug	dge lugs pa	Gelug sect

gen dun	dge 'dun	sangha
geshe	dge bshes	scholar
gri za	dri za	gandharva
gur	mgur	doha
gyü	gyud	tantra
gyu lama	rgyud bla ma	Uttaratantra
jampa	byams pa	Maitreya
yang	dbyangs	Manjushri
je trak ma wa	bye brag smra ba	Vaibhashika
ji nye pa	ji snyed pa	wisdom of variety
ji ta ba	ji lta ba	wisdom of phenomena
ka	ka	the Buddha's words
Kadam	bka' gdams	Kadam sect
kagyu	bka' brgyud	Kagyu sect
kangyur	bka' 'gyur	Kangyur
karma kagyu	karma bka' brgyud	Karma Kagyu
Karmapa	karma pa	Karmapa
khenpo	mkhan po	abbot
kor lo gyur pa	'khor los bsgyur ba	cakravartin
khorwa	'khor ba	samsara
kun sop	kun rdzop	conventional wisdom
ku sum	sku gsum	kayas three
kunshi namshe	kun gzhi' rnam shes	alaya consciousness
kye che	skye mched	ayatanas
lam lnga	lam lnga	five paths
lama	bla ma	guru
lay	las	karma
lha	lha	god
lha ma yin	lha ma yin	jealous god
lhag tong	lhag mthog	vipashyana
long ku	longs sku	sambhogakaya
ludrup	klu sgup	Nagarjuna
Marpa	mar pa	Marpa
mi bskyod pa	mi bskyod pa	Akshobhya
nam shé	rnam shes	consciousness
nam shé tsog gye	rnam shes tshogs brguad	consciousness, eight
neten depa	gnas brtan pa' sde	Theravada
ngedon	nges don	definitive meaning
ngo wo nyi kyi ku	ngo bo nyid sku	svabhavikakaya
nyangde	myang 'das	nirvana
nyan tho	nyan thos	shravaka
nyingma	rning ma	Nyingma sect
nyön m[illegible]	gnyon mongs	klesha

nyön yi	nyon yid	klesha consciousness
pak chak	bag chags	latencies
pak pay den pa shi	'phags pa'i bden pa bzhi	4 Noble Truths
parol tu chinpa	phar phyin drug	six paramitas
phag na mo	phag na mo	imperceivable particles
pung po	pung po	skandha
rang jung dorje	rang byung rdo rje	Rangjung Dorje
rang rig	rang rig	self-aware
rang sang gye	rang sangs rgyas	pratyekabuddha
rik druk	rigs drug gi skye gnas	6 realms of samsara
rinchen jungné	rin chen 'byang ldon	Ratnasambhava
rinpoche	rin po che	precious jewel
sa	sa	bodhisattva level
sakya	sa skya	Sakya sect
samten shi	bsam gtan bzhi	four concentrations
salwa	gsal ba	luminosity
sem	sems	mind
sem tam	sems tsam	Cittamatra school
shakya tubpa	sha kya thub pa	Buddha Shakyamuni
shentong	gzhan stong	Shentong school
sherab	shes rab	prajna
sherab chi patol ta chin pa	shes rab kyi phar phyin	Prajnaparamita
shinay	zhi gnas	shamatha
tenchö	bstan bcos	shastra
tek pa	theg pa	yana
tek pa chen po	theg pa chen po	Mahayana
tek pa chung wa	theg pa chung ba	Hinayana
tendrel	rten 'brel	dependent origination
tengyur	bstan' gyur	Tengyur
terma	gter ma	hidden treasure
thok mé	thogs med	Asanga
ji ta ba	ji lta ba	wisdom how it is
tin ne zin	ting nge 'dzin	samadhi
tong pa nyi	stong pa nyid	emptiness
tsa	rtsa	subtle channels
tse ma	tshad ma	pramana
tulku	sprul sku	nirmanakaya
u ma	dbu ma pa	Madhyamaka
yeshe	ye shes	wisdom
yeshe nga	ye shes lnga	five wisdoms
yi	yid	mind
yid shin norbu	yid bzhin gyi nor bu	wish-fulfilling jewel
yidik	yid dvags	hungry ghost

yi kyi namshay	yid kyi rnam shes	mental consciousness
yik nyen	dbyig gnyen	Vasubandhu
ying	dbyings	space
zug ku	gzugs sku	form body
zug kham	gzugs khams	form realm
zug me kham	gzugs med khams	formless realm

Annotated Bibliography

An Adornment for Rangjung Dorje's Thoughts by Jamgon Kongtrul. This is a commentary on Rangjung Dorje's *Distinguishing Consciousness from Wisdom* and has not been translated into English.

The Buddha Within by S. K. Hookham. Albany: State Univeristy of New York Press, 1991. Hookham gives an extensive commentary on the Shentong point of view of Buddha-nature. She also translates part of Jamgon Kongtrul's commentary on the Uttara Tantra.

A Handbook of Tibetan Culture by Graham Coleman. London: Rider, 1993. This book lists a great number of Buddhist centers around the world, gives biographies of many Tibetan lamas, and has an excellent glossary.

The Holographic Universe by Michael Talbot. Harper and Collins, 1991. This book summarizes the evidence that everything in the universe is related to everything else in the same manner that a small portion of a hologram contains the information on the entire object, but in less detail. He suggests that human awareness is similar to a laser which is the light source for the physical hologram.

The Hundred Thousand Songs of Milarepa. (Tib. *mila khabum*) by Tsang Myon Heruka translated into English by Chang, Garma C. C., trans. Secaucus, New Jersey, University Books, 1962. Milarepa was one of the greatest yogis to have ever lived. He taught by singing spontaneous spiritual songs and this is a collections of such teachings.

The King of Samadhi by the Buddha. (Skt. *Samadhi-raja-sutra).* This is one of the few teachings of the Buddha that discusses mahamudra meditation. The first four chapters of this sutra has been translated by John Rockwell at Naropa Institute and the eleventh chapter was translated by Mark Tatz in his Ph.D. thesis at the University of Washington. Thrangu Rinpoche has given an extensive commentary on this sutra in the *King of Samadhi.* Boudhanath, Nepal: Rangjung Yeshe Publications, 1994.

Masters of Mahamudra :Songs and Histories of the Eighty-Four Buddhist Siddhas by Keith Dowman. Albany, NY: State University of New York Press, 1985. Keith Dowman translats and gives an extensive commentary on the work by Abhayadatta who collected and wrote about eighty-four mahasiddhas.

Perfection of Wisdom Literature by the Buddha. There is a Prajnaparamita text of 100,000 verses, a text of 25,000 verses, a text of 8,000 verses, the Heart sutra of only a few verses right on down to a single seed syllable AH. The *Perfection of Wisdom* in 8,000 verses (Skt. *ashtasahasrika-prajna-paramita-sutra*, Tib. *'phag pa shes rab kyi pha rol tu phyin pa brgyad stron pa'i mdo*) has been translated by Edward Conze. *The Large Sutra on Perfect Wisdom*. Berkeley: University of California Press, 1975.

The Practice of Tranquillity and Insight by Thrangu Rinpoche. Ithaca, NY: Snow Lion Publications, 1993. This book gives an extensive treatment of meditation based on a chapter by Jamgon Kongtrul's *Treasury of Knowledge*.

The Profound Inner Meaning by Rangjung Yeshe. (Tib. *sabmo nang don*). This text is an explanation of the subtle channels and energies that move within them and how this relates to meditation.

The Self-Aware Universe: How Consciousness Creates the Material World by Amit Goswami. New York: Putnam, 1993. This book summarizes a number of modern experiments in physics that show that human consciousness or awareness is necessary for determining the characteristics of matter at least at an atomic level.

The Stages of Meditation by Kamalashila (Skt. *bhavanakrama*, Tib. *sgom pa'i rim pa*). This text in three volumes was written by Kamalashila (8th century C.E.) and laid the foundation for teaching the gradual path in Tibetan Buddhism. The first book was translated by Giuseppe Tucci in *Minor Buddhist Texts*, Part II. Serie Orientale Roma, IX.2. Rome: Is. M. E. O., 1958.

The Tantra of the Vajra View.
This text has not been translated into English.

The Tibetan Book of the Dead (Tib. *bard do'i thos grol*, pronounced *bardo thodrol*) This text was composed by Padmasambhava and written down by his wife Yeshe Tsogyal and hidden as a hidden treasure (Tib. *terma*). It was uncovered by Karma Lingpa. It is a text for achieving liberation while in the bardo state between death and a new rebirth. The first translation was by Evans-Wentz, the second was by Francesca Fremantle and Chogyam Trungpa Rinpoche and a recent version has been published by Robert Turman. See Fremantle and Trungpa, *The Tibetan Book of the Dead*. Boston: Shambhala, 1987.

The Treasury of the Abhidharma by Vasubandhu. (Skt. *abhidharma-kosha*, Tib. *chos mngon pa'i mdzod*). Vasubandhu great summary and commentary on the Abhidharma. This text was greatly respected in Tibet and is the main text used to study the abhidharma. A detailed study of this work has been published by Sukomal Chaudhuri in his *Analytical Study of the Abhidharmakosa* (Calcutta: Firma KLM, 1983).

The Treatise Distinguishing Consciousness from Wisdom by Rangjung Dorje (Tib. rnam shes ye shes 'byed pa, pronounced *namshe yeshe gepa*).

The Treatise Elucidating Buddha-Nature by Rangjung Dorje. This is a short spiritual song written by Rangjung Dorje that summarizes the teachings on buddha-nature. See *A Treatise Elucidating Buddha-nature* containing a translation of this spiritual song and a commentary by Thrangu Rinpoche (Boulder: Namo Buddha Publications, 1996).

The Upanishads. These are about one hundred Hindu religious texts dating from the seventh century B.C.E. One of the earliest and most important Upanishads was the Brihadavanyaka written in prose and concerned with the nature of the universe. These have been translated several times into English. See Alistair Shearer and Peter Russell. *The Upanishads*. New York: Harper and Row, 1978.

The Uttara Tantra by Maitreya (Skt. *ratnagotravibhaga*, Tib. *rgyud bla ma*, pronounced *gyu lama*). This text was written by Asanga in Sanskrit in about the fourth century who received a transmission from the bodhisattva Maitreya. For a translation of this text and a commentary by Thrangu Rinpoche see *The Uttara Tantra: A treatise on Buddha-nature* (Boulder: Namo Buddha Publications, 1999.

Table 6

The Bodhisattva Levels

1. The Joyous One (rab tu dga' ba) (rab tu dga' ba)	Emphasis on generosity (sbyin pa)
2. The Stainless One (dri ma med pa)	Emphasis on discipline (tsultrim)
3. The Illuminating One ('od byed pa)	Emphasis on patience (bzod pa)
4. The Flaming One ('od 'phro ba)	Emphasis on exertion (bzod pa)
5. The One Difficult to Conquer (shin tu sbyang dka' ba)	Emphasis on samadhi
6. The Manifest One (mngon du gyur ba)	Emphasis on wisdom (sherab)
7. The Far Going one activity (ring du song pa)	Emphasis on skilful (thabs la mkhas pa).
8. The Unshakable One (mi gyo ba) (smob lam)	Emphasis on future projection
9. The One of Good Discrimination (legs pa'i blo gros)	Emphasis on efficacy (stobs)
10. Cloud of Dharma (chos kyi sprin)	Attaining enlightened wisdom (ye shes)

INDEX